The term "Raggald" is a local Queensbury wor
for a Villain, Rapscallion or Ruffian.

The Jack Russell Terrier is an assertive, feisty,
loyal and intelligent, their assertive nature ar
be overwhelming. They require an extraordi
outdoor activity, exercise, discipline, and above all understanding and
patience.

These walks were completed between December 26 2016 and March 28 2017 and all within a radius of three and a half miles maximum from the centre of Queensbury. The length varies from 3.0 miles to 6.0 miles.

The front cover photograph depicts the author overlooking Shibden Brook at Sim Carr Clough deep in the Shibden Valley.

Copyright 2017 Mark Alexander Jackson All rights reserved worldwide. No part of this publication may be replicated, distributed or given away in any form without the prior written consent of the author/publisher.

This book is dedicated to the ten men who lost their lives during the construction of the Queensbury Railway Tunnel (1874-1878)

Forward

I have always had the ability to know when something has come to its true and natural end. Be it a job, relationship, family or a marriage, when the end comes it comes and you have to let it go.

I had enjoyed seventeen good years as the custodian of a beautiful old cottage in Wrose, but now with the stroke of a pen it belonged to someone else. I use the term custodian as although I owned it in a legal sense I merely cared for it until the next owner came along.

I had no ties to bind me, only my trusty Jack Russell Lou Parson, some books and an old computer. The notion of being able to live anywhere you please is an empowering feeling and I considered many places, some with merit and some completely barmy. The only criteria I set myself was that it had to inspire me in a historical sense and be close to the broader Calderdale area. The reason for this was I had completed four of the historical walks for a book based on the Calderdale area and had developed an affinity with the area.

Over the previous four years, during the walks for my previous books I had visited some fantastically historic and inspiring villages and hamlets. The wider Bradford, Wharfedale and Leeds areas are overflowing with such places. I thought about where I would make my future home so much that it became a montage of images swimming around my head. But one image always had more clarity that any of the others.

Three years previously I had struggled up the steep ancient footpath leading from the floor of Bradford-dale up to Sandbeds. Gasping for breath, I turned around just as the cloud above drifted away towards Bradford and as it did so it released the sun from its shackles. The life-giving ball of fire was now free to illuminate the landscape before me, and it didn't disappoint as it brought life to what I now know to be the Railway Triangle.

Lou Parson and I had just walked across from Thornton so I was well aware of the inspiring beauty and historical importance of the land before me. This one brief moment was to leave an indelible mark on my very soul and it was this image that kept playing in my mind.

So I made my plans, said my goodbyes and came to live in Queensbury.

Oh yes, and I wrote another book.

Chapters

1) Ancient Trails and Walled Gardens — 5
2) Clayton Village and an Ancient Corn Mill — 13
3) Queensbury to Beggarington via Bradshaw — 23
4) Walking in the Shadow of the Fosters — 30
5) A Brewery and a Beck — 37
6) Shibden Dale and Black Boy House — 44
7) Littlemoor and the Spirit of Elgar — 53
8) Hanging Falls and the Hill of Squirrels — 61
9) Brow Top Mill and Clayton Railway Tunnel — 68
10) The Old Man on the Mountain — 76
11) Standing on Top of the World — 83
12) A Salute to Mr Benton and Mr Woodiwiss — 91

Ancient Trails and Walled Gardens

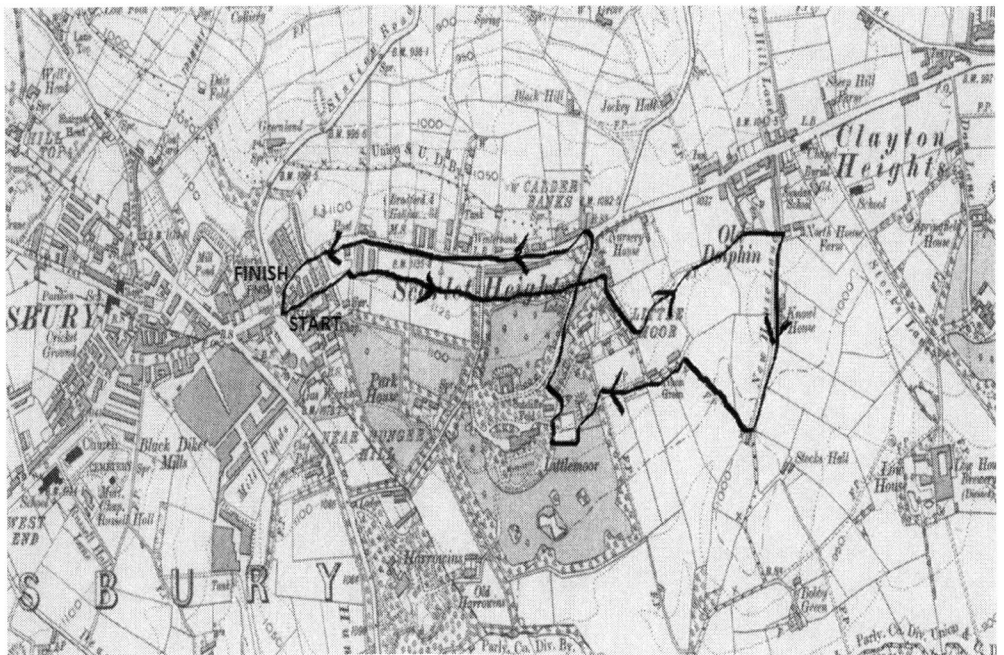

For a village of its size, importance, and character, Queensbury is unusual in that it is a relatively recent settlement when compared to many villages or even hamlets in the district. There is no record of any settlement until after 1750 and before this date the site of the village would have been no more than scrubland and desolate moorland. The high and exposed location prevented any permanent habitation with only the most basic of tracks and footpaths encroaching upon what was at best, an inhospitable area.

The moorland which would one day be the centre of Queensbury was bisected by the boundary which separated the ancient ecclesiastical parishes of Bradford and Halifax, the Manors of Bolton (Bradford parish) and Wakefield (Halifax parish), and the townships of Clayton and Northowram. The catalyst for the establishment of the village was the construction of a turnpike between Bradford and Halifax.

The turnpike, a route which remains unchanged to this very day, was completed in 1740, with the site of Queensbury as its highest point with the end of the improved surface running down to Bradford and an unmade track completing the route's descent in the opposite direction to Halifax.

The area of the present-day High Street in Queensbury became known as Causeway End due to the change in the road surface. The main purpose of this route was to transport wool and cloth to the Piece Halls in Bradford and Halifax.

Prior to the construction of the Turnpike road the Sandbeds area was accessed by two ancient rights of way. One, known as Deep Lane roughly follows the route of the road to Brighouse over Hunger Hill before it was realigned to its present-day course in 1824. The present day path, partly surfaced with tarmac, runs through rough unkempt grassland and links to the west ends of Victoria Street and Albert Street in the Brickfields estate. Deep Lane is still a handy shortcut for reaching the village centre from Brickfields and for some time led to Foster's brickworks hence the name.

The Brickfields Estate, built by John Foster and Son to house their mill workers was constructed in 1850-52. It contains a combination of back-to-back and through terraces with a mixture of two and three levels which reflects different phases of development by the Fosters. The design of the houses changes from row to row but they are united by their use of stone and stone slates, plain decoration, similar heights and roof slopes.

This development incorporated shop fronts to the properties along Sandbeds, though most of these are now private houses with the segmental heads to the large former shop windows remaining. A notable survival is that of a former co-op branch, which today trades as "The Handyman". The timber frame to the front has been retained to give a very attractive and traditional shop front.

The second ancient track terminates between numbers 28 and 30 Sandbeds and is squeezed between the back of Wellington Street (the edge of the Brickfields estate) and the older buildings along the main road. Although it starts as a "Ginnel", this pathway opens up as it runs parallel to Sandbeds and continues for some distance beyond Scarlet Heights and down towards Clayton Heights.

It was here that I stood on a cold but bright Wednesday afternoon in early February. The heady aroma of sizzling bacon wafting out from nearby Maguire's sandwich shop made me glad that I had eaten before setting out from home. Gazing up at the entrance of the disused workshop facility for the nearby Black Dyke Mills, I was hoping that my mind would be filled with vivid images of hooded men struggling through the mud with their sweating Packhorses lined up behind them. The beast's hot breath hanging heavy in the cold winter air, the ground beneath their hooves matted with thick mud and straw from the nearby stables of the Halfway House. Travellers, Monks, Merchants and even the odd Raggald all used this trail to struggle up the incline from the pastures down below.

Sadly the empty beer cans and general modern day detritus at this end of the footpath made me struggle to engage my imagination in its usual manner, but I was not alarmed as I knew things would get better as I travelled towards Scarlet Heights.

After gently avoiding the large piles of dog muck, Lou Parson and I set off to retrace the steps of the simple hooded men from times long ago. After only a few feet I came to the rear of the Halfway House pub. Named so for its location halfway between Halifax and Bradford it has been a popular and welcome sight for travellers for two centuries or more. The rear yard and smoking area were once the location of the stables and certain associated artefacts can still be seen as you fill your lungs with nicotine. Here, horses and ponies would be stabled, rested and fed and even exchanged for those that had struggled up the hillside so that the journey down the other side to Halifax could be completed. Known at one time as the Virgin Mary and later as The Wellington, the pub has now reverted to its most popular moniker of The Halfway House. The Landlord in 1901 had the most wonderful name of "Christmas Staff".

Seriously, it wasn't an advert in the window for bar help over the festive period it was the Landlords name!

It was my intention to follow this ancient right of way for as long as I could. To this end, I crossed Brunswick Street and continued past the rear of humble mill workers cottages, then across Lyon Street till I reached the end of the streets of Stone Leigh and Fern Lea. Here the cobbles became more evident and uneven and this started to give me a stronger feeling of how the path would have appeared two centuries ago. But within a few yards, the past had evaporated once again to be replaced by modern day tarmac and more dog crap. The signs proclaiming death and eternal damnation to all who allow their dogs to foul along this stretch are obviously disregarded it seems. Just why Lou Parson has to stop and examine every single bit is known only to her-it's a dog thing apparently.

The footpath continued through the modern houses of the Naseby estate before Lou and I crossed Park Road and started to skirt along the edge of Littlemoor estate. Here the surface degenerated into thick cloying mud and any thoughts of avoiding the dog mess were abandoned so we simply slogged on forward. Stopping for a moment, I stood on tiptoes to glance over the fence across the expanse of parkland towards the site of Littlemoor's long gone Coach House. Perhaps the village urchins clad in their raggy clothes will have stood on this exact spot to catch a glimpse of the favoured life enjoyed by those who lived within the estate.

The Coach House and stables were used to house the carriages, carts, and horses that served the grand house of Littlemoor nearby. It was also used as a Fire Station during 1939-1945 war. The 1911 census shows one George Shaw (age 57 Coachman) and his wife Elizabeth Shaw (age 62) residing here with their two grown children John and Mary.

As I peered over the high stone wall surrounding the estate, Lou Parsons's usual high pitched bark (or yap as none Jack Russell owners call it) alerted me to a rapidly advancing figure along the path. The young girl was struggling with a rather large and muscular Boxer that was dragging her along through the mud towards us. My instinct told me this dog harboured only good and playful intentions as it appeared quite young, but I have learnt over the years to play it safe where my dogs have been concerned and as we were hemmed in by the wall and a large fence overlooking the rear of Upper Fawth Close, I decided to take evasive action. This involved simply picking Lou up and holding her above my head as the girl and the Boxer passed us by. But nothing is ever that simple with a Jackie Russell.

To be honest this action was more to prevent Lou acting hard with the larger dog as the Jack Russell often does this when it is confronted. I held her above my head as she flailed and thrashed to escape from my grip and get at the Boxer. It was like standing in front of a muck spreader in as she plastered me with most of the mud she had picked up along the way from Sandbeds. The young girl giggled all the way back to Park Lane and never looked back once whilst I made plans for a good bath.

After this little interlude, I had become a little bored of trudging through the mud so was relieved when the muck spreader and I reached the estate Lodge. Along with Harrowins Lodge at the far end of Park Lane, this marvellous building is still occupied today, and as small as it is the dwelling gives an indication of the grandeur in which the Foster family lived. It was here that the trees on the estate ended and the track became somewhat more substantial as it led to a small clutch of estate workers cottages named Littlemoor.

As I passed the cottages I caught a glimpse of two grey haired old women sat in the window of one of the cottages. They were drinking tea and chatting about past times when life on Littlemoor estate was simpler and purer no doubt.

The track continued on towards the cottages of Tilson Green which were originally two cottages but were converted into one in the 1980's by the present owner I believe. I quickly spied the ancient packhorse trail and footpath once again and passing through the rickety gate, I headed for the area marked on the old maps as Old Dolphin. It was here that the landscape changed from mature trees and woodland to more open pasture.

From here the mud had been replaced by a grassier surface under foot which was due to the more open surroundings. The sun made its first appearance of the day and this brightened my mood greatly as Lou and I walked along the gently undulating path towards the simple but beautiful "Lowdecker" cottages at the end of Stogden Hill. These basic but sturdy dwellings were constructed for local quarry workers and labourers and are dotted all around South Bradford due to the high number of tiny Delfs or quarries that existed in the area.

It was here that my journey along the ancient packhorse trail ended. I joined New House Lane, and here the green fields and pastures really opened up. After stopping to remove the copious amounts of mud from my boots I headed south towards another footpath which would take me back over the fields towards Tilson Green once again.

New House Lane gives access to North House Farm, Knowl House, Stocks Hall and the farmstead of Bobby Green, before becoming Blackshaw Beck Lane as it crosses the beck of the same name. At the side of some well used allotments I looked back over the undulating pasture towards the dense canopy of aged trees that still cover the estate of Littlemoor. The view that my eyes enjoyed will not have changed one bit in over two centuries.

The onset of Trench foot from the mud was still a distinct possibility as I started along the short footpath that covered the fields across to Tilson Green. The ground was saturated by a nearby spring that like the many other springs in the area will have permutated the ground with life-giving water for millennia. The water from this spring runs gently away to join Blackshaw Beck some 450 metres away. But I had a more pressing problem at this point as Lou and I were being watched from afar. She had sensed this long before I had and had stopped in a pool of water to return the stare across the field.

Our observer was a distant man standing on the edge of a building just along the track from Tilson Green. He continued to watch us like a hawk as we crossed the field and finally entered the track by the farm. Even though we had been on a public footpath the man had not once taken his eyes off us. I feared a tongue lashing for straying onto parts of land that were private but I was ready with my retort as I knew no laws or rules had been broken. His two large dogs thankfully stayed in his garden but they followed Lou and I as we skirted past his residence. He was not happy with our intrusion as it was all he could do to offer a gruff "alright" as we drew level. Only a few more steps I thought then we are past him and back into the field. For once I was glad that Lou was pulling like a train and the difficult moment evaporated.

The dense trees of Littlemoor Park stood but a short distance away and it was here that I mounted a wire fence and literally fell into the park. Lou Parson was already through and in hot pursuit of something moving and edible. So naturally I was pulled on my knees through the mud until a large Holly bush stopped the dog's fun. But as luck would have it we had appeared in the park right at the site of what was once a small Sandstone quarry. Well, it wasn't exactly a quarry more of a small Delf, but the sunken nature of the ground and the fact that it was marked on my Smartphone OS map as a Delf told me exactly what it was.

The Delf was used to provide stone for the surrounding walls of the estate. When it had outlived its usefulness it was abandoned and gradually filled with water. After a young local boy drowned it was drained and filled in with rubbish and became known by some as "Patchett's Tip".

Every great country house and estate enjoyed its own walled garden and Littlemoor was no exception. The magnificent sturdy red brick walls still stand today as a testament to the skill and endeavours of the estate gardeners that were employed by the estate. This once bountiful Garden of Eden is today sadly overgrown and abandoned, its healthy and vibrant harvests belonging to a distant long forgotten age. Once providing the nearby mansion with all manner of edible delights, the garden now supplies numerous woodland creatures with their homes and habitats. As a part of the large estate, this garden would have been a highly productive area supplying the big house with fruit, vegetables, herbs, and flowers. The regimented layouts were purely functional and contained specific areas for each edible plant.

The high red brick walls provided protection from predators and the elements and also created a micro-climate within. The heat retained by the walls helped in the production of fruit on trees trained against them. Along the South facing wall of walled gardens such as this would usually stand a line of glasshouses and forcing sheds, some of them heated. Here the growing season could be extended and exotic species of fruit and vegetables could be produced.

Titus Salt Jnr's magnificent Gothic revival Victorian mansion at Milner Field near Saltaire enjoyed the benefits of the first Pineapple tree in England in its garden complex. The fruit was even offered to Queen Victoria it was that unusual for the period. At Littlemoor there was a banana tree but that was kept in the Conservatory.

The walled garden at Littlemoor did indeed enjoy the presence of a long glasshouse that ran the whole length of the South facing wall. The supporting brackets for the roof joists can still be clearly seen as can the access door in the wall itself. Sadly today the walled kitchen garden is unloved, forlorn and securely locked up tight so there was no chance I could have a look around inside.

But it can be true that when one door closes another one opens. So imagine my joy when I rounded the corner of the walled garden and stumbled upon a quite magnificent row of cottages named Sutcliffe Fold. These humble dwellings predate the main house of Littlemoor and were used to house estate workers such as gardeners. The 1911 census shows Martin Rawson (age 34 Head Gardener), Alice Parr (age 53 Housekeeper), Ernest James Lane (age 34 second Gardener), Matthew Bosomworth (Butler), Bessie Gertrude

Bosomworth (age 33) and Elizabeth Kathleen Bosomworth (age 1) as residing there. One of the cottages was even used to house Belgian refugees during the First World War.

Time had overtaken me by now and the sun had disappeared to leave behind a poor quality available light. My feet were wet and my boots squelching with every step so I was rather happy to be heading home. I couldn't face another bout of dancing around like a loony to avoid the dog mess on the ancient footpath so with this in mind I headed out of the estate towards the main road, home, and a warm bath.

Clayton Village and An Ancient Corn Mill

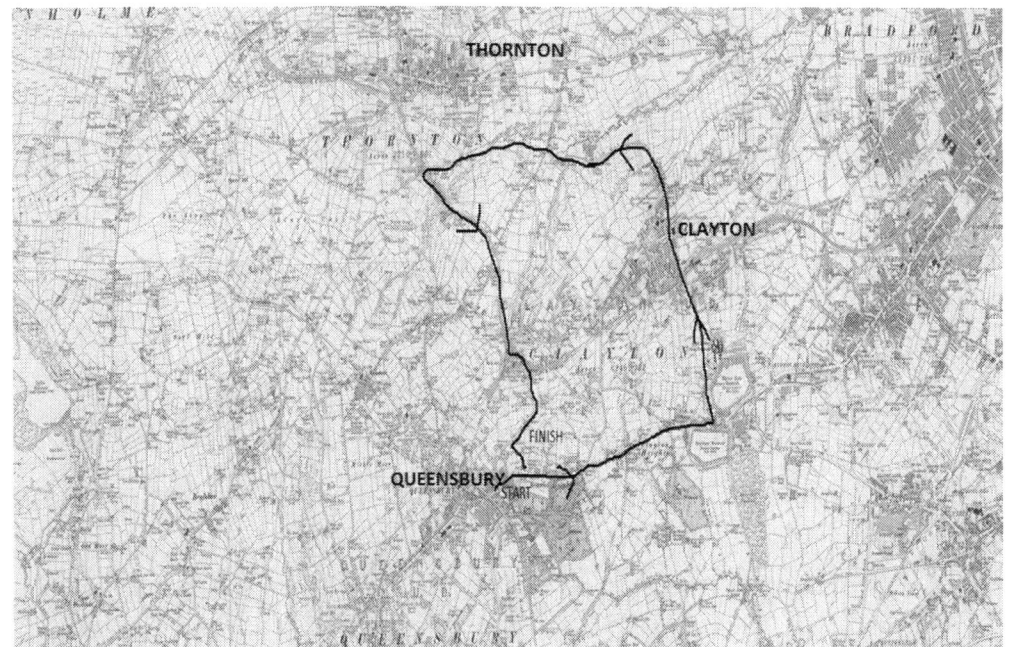

Nothing excites me more than the prospect of wandering around the site of a long disappeared grand house and estate or even an old mill. So when I noticed the words "Corn mill" on the 1888-1913 Ordnance Survey map my interest was suitably aroused. It was not too far away so I dug around and found some other places of interest and it ultimately developed into this walk.

Friday the third of February dawned with the sky covered in low cloud that promised to float away to reveal bright sunshine later in the morning. So I took my time doing the things I do in a morning at home then set off just before lunchtime. With the ever ready Lou Parson at my side as usual I set off along Sandbeds heading for Horton Bank Top. This initial part of the walk slipped by quickly as the downhill direction compelled Lou Parson to dictate the pace somewhat. I had to be content with being dragged along by the feisty Terrier.

After a short and brisk stroll I found myself stood before the magnificent sandstone entrance arch to what was once Highgate Mill. Constructed in 1865 it was occupied by Henry Briggs and Co and others before being acquired by the Jewish Textile magnate Solomon Selka. The Grade II listed 2.27-acre site has recently been converted into modern apartments but the large ashlar entrance portal of this former woolen spinning mill remains and stands guard over the modest homes within the courtyard beyond.

A more detailed look around this captivating building would have to wait for another time as I had a long way to go and much to see. So with that notion in mind I once again set off and before long I turned down the side of the ancient village Smithy and along Union House Lane. The next destination was of course the famous and imposing former workhouse, and with thoughts of the many tortured souls that suffered there floating around my head, I headed to confront them. In a spiritual way of course.

But before reaching the site of the former workhouse I had to skirt around the edge of Horton Bank Country Park. This site was once one of the most famous stone quarries in Bradford with many of the neighboring houses being built from its stone. In 1871, plans were drawn up to turn this quarry into a reservoir and these were accepted with building work starting later that year. It was finished just three years later and was to become a vital aid in the provision of drinkable water for the people of Bradford

The reservoir supplied water to the city every day for over a century, but in the 1980s a secret safety report concluded that hundreds of people down in Clayton were under threat of a deadly flood. An inspection had discovered that the earth dam showed major structural problems. They also found that the culvert which would take the water away in an emergency was blocked with tons of silt. A landslide or earth movement would endanger the villagers below as 150 million gallons of water could potentially come their way.

The reservoir was closed in September 1989 when it became infected with bacterial algae. In November, Bradford West MP Max Madden brought the issue up in parliament to Michael Howard, the then Minister for Water & Planning, but Howard announced that he couldn't do anything and it was up to Yorkshire Water. In December 1990 plans were finally announced when planning permission was submitted for the construction of two temporary water storage tanks to serve as service reservoirs. This confirmed the idea held by most people that the reservoir was to be drained. This was followed up in 1992 by further permission to convert the reservoir into parkland.

Yorkshire Water paid £750,000 to convert the reservoir and the new Horton Bank Country Park was officially opened on 15 July 1997. It was designated as a Local Wildlife Site. Horton Bank Country Park contains a lake as well as walkers' route and is a fantastic way to spend an hour or two. The lake attracts many varieties of wildlife and waterfowl and the park has become a walkers' favorite with a beautiful panoramic view of Bradford.

Back across Highgate Road a second reservoir, opened in 1871, named Brayshaw Reservoir also provided water to the city of Bradford but today this area contains modern housing and only the stone entrance pillars remain.

The wonderful whitewashed cottage of Nab End stands at the end of Union House Road and here the access road to the former workhouse site changes to a steep tarmac track which passes by former filter beds on one side and the heavy vegetation and sturdy high retaining wall of the country park on the other.

The North Bierley Workhouse at Clayton was built in 1855-8 by the firm of Henry F Lockwood and William Mawson to accommodate the rapidly growing city of Bradford, which was starting to have to deal with large numbers of poor people. It was designed to accommodate up to 400 inmates but as usual for these kinds of places ended up housing many more.

Converted to a hospital called "Thornton View" in 1948, the workhouse eventually became a private girls school in 1991. Interestingly from 1904 onwards, the address given for all birth registrations was number 1 Highgate Road, Clayton. This was to protect children born there from the shame of being registered as being born in a workhouse. The reason for this was to prevent them from being stigmatized later in life.

North Bierley workhouse had a two storey entrance building to the East with a central archway with a further block attached to its Western end. The three storey T-shaped main building accommodated females in the North and males in the South. The central wing at the rear contained the dining hall and kitchens and formed the northern side of an enclosed yard. A bake-house, laundry and boiler house lay beyond with the original Infirmary to the North West.

The workhouse was enlarged in 1907, and later additions to the southwest included a further infirmary block and a nurse's home. The original infirmary black was converted for use a mental block, with the addition of circular padded cells at its rear. If you were unlucky enough to be confined in a workhouse the view was that you couldn't be picky. You were supposed to be grateful for what you got, even if it wasn't much.

The origins of the workhouse can be traced to the Poor Law Act of 1388, which attempted to address the labour shortages following the Black Death in England by restricting the movement of laborers. This ultimately led to the state becoming responsible for the support of the poor. But mass unemployment following the end of the Napoleonic Wars in 1815, the introduction of new technology to replace agricultural workers, and a series of bad harvests, meant that by the early 1830s the established system of poor relief was proving to be unsustainable.

The New Poor Law of 1834 attempted to reverse the economic trend by discouraging the provision of relief to anyone who refused to enter a workhouse. Some Poor Law authorities hoped to run workhouses at a profit by utilizing the free labour of their inmates, who generally lacked the skills or motivation to compete in the open market. Most were employed on tasks such as breaking stones, crushing bones to produce fertilizer, or picking oakum by using a large metal nail known as a spike.

Life in a workhouse was intended to be harsh. This would hopefully deter the able-bodied poor and ensure that only the truly destitute would apply. But in areas such as the provision of free medical care and education for children, neither of which was available to the poor in England living outside workhouses until the early 20th century, workhouse inmates were advantaged over the general population, a dilemma that the Poor Law authorities never managed to reconcile.

As the 19th century wore on, workhouses increasingly became refuges for the elderly, infirm and sick rather than the able-bodied poor, and in 1929 legislation was passed to allow local authorities to take over workhouse infirmaries and run them as municipal hospitals. Although workhouses were formally abolished by the same legislation in 1930, many continued under their new appellation of Public Assistance Institutions under the control of local authorities. It was not until the National Assistance Act of 1948 that the last vestiges of the Poor Law disappeared, and with them the workhouses.

In 1836 the Poor Law Commission distributed six diets for workhouse inmates, one of which was to be chosen by each Poor Law Union depending on its local circumstances. Although dreary, the food was generally nutritionally adequate, and according to contemporary records was prepared with great care. Issues such as training staff to serve and weigh portions were well understood. The diets included general guidance, as well as schedules for each class of inmate. They were laid out on a weekly rotation with the various meals selected on a daily basis from a list of foodstuffs. For instance, a breakfast of bread and gruel was followed by dinner, which might consist of cooked meats, pickled pork or bacon with vegetables, potatoes, yeast dumpling, soup and suet, or rice pudding. Supper was normally bread, cheese and broth, and sometimes butter or potatoes.

The larger workhouses had separate dining rooms for males and females; workhouses without separate dining rooms would stagger the meal times to avoid any contact between the sexes. Rations provided for the indoor staff were much the same as those for the paupers, although more generous. The master and matron, for instance, received six times the amount of food given to a pauper.

Discipline was strictly enforced in the workhouse. For minor offences such as swearing or feigning sickness the "disorderly" could have their diet restricted for up to 48 hours. For more serious offences such as insubordination or violent behaviour the "refractory" could be confined for up to 24 hours, and might also have their diet restricted. Girls were punished in the same way as adults, but boys under the age of 14 could be beaten with "a rod or other instrument, such as may have been approved of by the Guardians". The persistently refractory, or anyone bringing "spirituous or fermented liquor" into the workhouse, could be taken before a Justice of the Peace and even jailed.

As I sat on a high stone wall opposite the entrance, I remembered a tale recounted to me three summers previously by an old woman that I had met whilst walking high above Thornton village. Her gnarled and wizened old face grimaced with sadness as she told me the story of her long dead relative who sadly ended his days in the building before me.

Eli Anderton was born in the Lightcliffe area, near Halifax in 1808, the son of James and Sarah Anderton. He married Mary Cryer in 1832 at Halifax. Mary was heavily pregnant at the time, and was the daughter of James Cryer, a farmer from Norwood Green near Halifax and his wife Frances. Looking at the census records, it would seem that Eli had a variety of occupations throughout his life. 1841 showed him as a farmer in Lightcliffe, while by 1851 he and his family had moved to Raistrick near Halifax and he was then shown as a wool comber.

By 1861 he had moved to Cleckheaton and was now working as an Agricultural Labourer and was widowed. Eli must have been a rather unpleasant character as far as his family was concerned as he appears to have started a six-month prison sentence shortly before his wife died at the early age of 46 years because he "inhumanly treated" her. One can only speculate whether her early death was due to having ten children or the cruel treatment at the hands of her husband.

Eli eventually ended his days in the North Bierley Union Workhouse and the 1871 census lists him there as an inmate, together with several hundred other unfortunate individuals. He is shown as being of sound mind and body, unlike some of the others there, who are described as "imbecile or deaf and dumb".

Sitting there on the warm stone of the wall I surmised that no matter how bad things get it simply cannot get as bad today as it did for the poor wretched souls who had to endure the Victorian Workhouse. I was still thanking my lucky stars as I guided Lou Parson along through the streets of the village of Clayton.

As we crossed the small roundabout in the village a young girl with four leashed Chihuahuas walked with some degree of difficulty along the pavement towards us. The Jack Russell is perfectly able and willing to stand and fight with just about any dog large or small, but four of these little monsters in a group would be a bit much even for Lou Parson. The opposite pavement seemed a much better idea to me so I quickly crossed over the road. The four mental Mexican amigos still made a beeline for us though and the young girl was literally dragged into the centre of the road as she struggled to contain them. The passing Morrisons delivery van only just missed us all.

On the right of Town End Road is a farmhouse and barn right on the roadside. The huge barn door was open and inside I could see a number of cows and the tarmac apron outside contained a large group of assorted Poultry. Lou of course made her usual attempt at a chicken dinner as we passed by and sent most of them clucking back inside the barn to join the cows. It was a rather bizarre scene as I had to remind myself I was on a fairly busy minor road in a village on the edge of the sixth largest city in England and not high up in the Yorkshire Dales.

By this time I had the familiar scent of a long-gone mill in my flaring nostrils. I was feeling the urge to cover the ground down the valley side towards Fall Bottom, Chat Hill and the site of what was once Thornton Corn Mill. So I didn't hang about (see what I did there?) as I passed Back Fold and number 14 which was once the residence of the famous Hangman Thomas Pierrepoint.

Thomas Pierrepoint began working as a hangman in 1906 under the influence of his brother, Henry. His career spanned 39 years, and ended in 1946, by which time he was in his mid-seventies. During this time, he is thought to have carried out 294 hangings, 203 of which were civilians executed in England and Wales, whilst the remainder were executions carried out abroad or upon military personnel.

In 1940, his medical fitness for the job was questioned by a Medical Officer who called him "unsecure" and doubted "whether his sight was good". The Prison Commission discreetly asked for reports on his performance during executions in the following time, but evidently found no reason to take action, although one report said that Thomas Pierrepoint had "smelled strongly of drink" on two occasions when reporting at the prison. This, however, appears to clash with Thomas Pierrepoint's instruction to Albert (when the latter acted as his assistant) not to take a drink if on the job and never to accept the drink customarily given to all witnesses at executions in the Republic of Ireland.

Thomas never officially "retired", rather his name was removed from the list of executioners and invitations to conduct executions ceased to arrive. He died at his daughter's home in Bradford on 11 February 1954, aged 83.

The traffic whizzed by at speed as Lou Parson and I descended Low lane towards Clayton Beck and the valley floor. Most of the vehicles appeared to be travelling at an illegal speed although after some years as an ex-driver it has now become somewhat difficult to judge such things with any degree of accuracy.

Until the late nineteenth century Clayton almost completely consisted of open green pasture land with very few buildings. Maps from as late as 1893 show mostly fields and very little else apart from the main village and isolated farmsteads. Between then and 1912 quite a lot of development seems to have taken place, but there was still much green land and, even today, Clayton is still separated by fields from its nearest neighbours, Thornton and Queensbury.

These same open green fields greeted Lou and I as we strode down Low Lane past the former sites of Clayton Gas Works, Albion Brewery and Low Lane Pit. The privately-owned gasworks was opened in 1865 and supplied Clayton, Thornton and Allerton. The Local Board took on the responsibility of laying pipes throughout the district, and the principal portion of Clayton Township was lit by gas for the first time on Christmas Eve 1873. The brewery once strangely enough owned the pub named The Albion back above in Clayton village.

Approaching Fall Bottom I stopped to consult the OS map of the area that I had downloaded to my Smartphone. I discovering that I was very close to Corn Mill Lane and this revelation only served to heighten my building excitement. I knew this site contained not only the beck that powered the old mill but also the remnants of the mill pond and Mill Race.

The terms "gristmill" or "corn mill" can refer to any mill that grinds grain. These names were historically used for a local mill where farmers brought their own grain and received back the ground meal or flour, minus a percentage called the miller's toll. Early mills were almost always built and supported by farming communities and the miller received the "miller's toll" in lieu of wages. The mill would be local so that local farmers could easily transport their grain there to be milled. These communities were dependent on their local mill as bread was a staple part of the diet.

Classical mill designs are usually water powered, though some are powered by the wind or by livestock. With a watermill, a sluice gate is opened to allow water to flow onto, or under, a water wheel to make it turn. In most watermills the water wheel was mounted vertically, i.e., edge-on, in the water, but in some cases horizontally (the tub wheel and so-called Norse wheel).

After a short walk down Corn Mill Lane, and ignoring the enquiring gaze from the bloke in the adjacent smallholding, I was slightly disappointed to discover that the site of the mill is now covered by what appeared to be a collection of shabby old sheds and assorted buildings. I didn't really expect to see a huge waterwheel spinning around with Windy Miller grinding his grist for all he was worth but I would like to have seen something. But I did expect to see the beck, pond and goit that once turned the waterwheel as it is visible on Google Earth, and it was to this area that Lou Parson and I now headed for.

The small beck that once drove the waterwheel is called Pinch Beck. It joins Clayton Beck some four hundred metres to the East from the field in which I now stood. Here the somewhat small but still powerful watercourse has cut its way through the earth for millennia and the thin channel runs through the meadow like a demented snake. It twists and turns and runs almost back on itself at one point as it carries the clear water away to ultimately join Bradford Beck and thence the river Aire at Shipley.

Crossing over the beck via a small stone clapper bridge, I followed the route for perhaps two hundred yards till I came to the point where the beck was originally diverted to form the Mill Race or Goit as it is sometimes known. Here a series of large stone slabs form a weir. The channel where the water once flowed to power the mill is today totally dry and water free but its trajectory can still be seen.

The site of the larger of the two mill ponds lies close by at this point. This would have held water ready for use when needed. The remnants of the stone retaining wall and a slight dip in the ground gives an indication as to the exact location of the pond. I was astounded that such a small area still held all this historical information and that it is still discernable if you know what to look for.

I had been wandering around this nondescript field for what seemed an age when I was abruptly brought to my senses by the approaching clatter of farm machinery. Not wanting to enrage the local farming folk I quickly reined in Lou Parson's leash and slinked off along the edge of the field towards the cottages at Green Lane Bottom.

It sometimes seems to me that the whole Queensbury area is populated by Jack Russells. Everywhere Lou Parson and I travel we come across members of this most delightful of dog breeds. Fantastic dogs they are and I should know as I have brought up five of the buggers and my life has been better for the experience. So, imagine my delight as we started up the steep gradient of Green lane, and upon passing the cottages at the bottom, found the front window of the centre cottage almost pushed out from its frame by a snarling and spitting male Jack.

Standing fully stretched on the window ledge, it appeared as though it was his whole life's ambition to reach us and tear us apart. His taught muscular legs propelled him up the glass as his snout drove a furrow through the snot and saliva on the cold glass. He was obviously enjoying himself in the peculiar way that these dogs do so I stood in the middle of the empty road with my arms folded admiring this wonderful spectacle being played out before me. Surely he would either lose interest or stamina before too long but not a chance as I could still hear him barking madly when I had reached the turn off for the railway trail five hundred yards away.

My ears were still ringing when I reached the top of the ancient footpath that ends between the former Doctors surgery of Craig-na-Hullie and Scarlet Heights Farm at Sandbeds. This property was originally established as a surgery before WW2 by Dr. Sharp who originated from Scotland and gave the house the name of Craig na Hullie. It continued to be used after Dr Sharp by a Dr. Glen and then by a Dr. Hainsworth until at least the early 1970's.

This is of course my favourite spot in the whole area, and as I stood there once more surveying the land before me just as the Victorian railway Engineers would have done all those years ago, I had a feeling of a job well done. Although I could not see the valley floor that I had walked along from Town End at Clayton to the edge of Thornton, I knew it was there, somewhere, beyond the vista that fed my straining eyes.

Queensbury To Beggarington Via Bradshaw

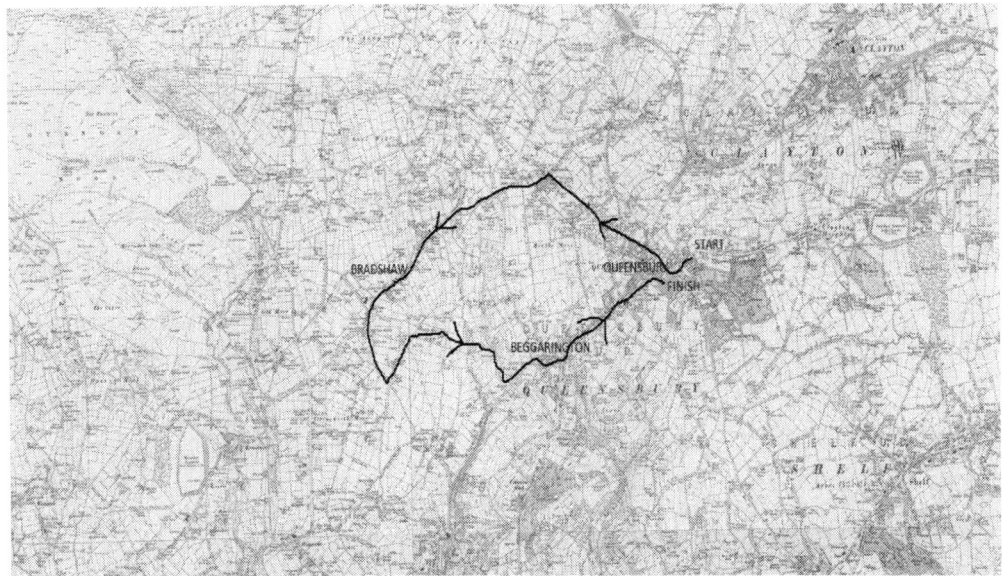

Tuesday the seventh of March dawned and brought with it the finest weather since I had come to live in Queensbury. I felt compelled to get out in the sun and feel the road and fields beneath my feet. To this end Lou Parson and I set off for what was to be our longest historical walk around the Queensbury area yet.

The walk out to our starting point at Raggalds was complicated only by the seemingly strategically placed piles of dog mess all the way through Mountain. At one point for over one hundred yards we played a surreal game of hopscotch in an attempt to avoid the Canine crap, but it got my leg muscles loose and working correctly though. Ye Olde Raggalds Inn (as it was once known) is thankfully a peaceful place these days, which after its somewhat chequered past is something of a relief. The former eighteenth-century farmhouse was known as a den for thieves and in the nineteenth-century villains met there to target travellers using the hilltop route.

It was also used for staging prize fights and wrestling matches and as a turnpike house where tolls were collected on the route from Queensbury. The pub was also reputed to be the birthplace of Jonas White, the Grandfather of the "Cats Eyes" reflective road studs inventor Percy Shaw.

The pub was soon behind us as we turned down Green Lane towards the many splendid roadside cottages in the village of Bradshaw. The ancient road is lined on one side by the sheep filled fields of Farsides Farm and open green pastures on the other. The high drystone walls funnelled Lou Parson and I downhill towards what was once Daniel Fielding's White Castle Brewery.

Today the site is no longer a brewery and has been converted into modern living accommodation. Worked for many years by Thornton born Fielding, the concern was sold to Webster's brewery in 1961. I was making good progress by now as the road was on something of an incline and naturally as usual the headstrong Lou Parson was dictating the pace. But I had to stop her with some difficulty when we came upon Bonnet Hall and the entrance to Taylor Lane. At this point the side road was constructed using what was possibly the finest collection of Setts that I had yet seen around this area. It is a shame that only the first eighty feet or so are covered in these fine granite stones which were widely used as they provided horses hooves with better grip than a smooth surface.

The village of Bradshaw has a beauty all of its own. The long straggling rows of cottages erected on each side of the winding road, the rugged boldness of the hills at the foot of which the village nestles and the scattered homesteads all have all a charm of their own. I didn't see one pile of dog mess from one end of the village to the other until Lou Parson decided to create a piece of her own pavement art. Naturally I picked it up and deposited the firm small bullets in a nearby bin.

The farms around this area are intersected with footpaths, and even some of the side roads partake of the primitive character of the place, having the look of simple bridle paths as they cut through the landscape. In places along the main street the eighteenth-century setts beneath the modern day tarmac can still be clearly seen along the edges.

Most villages and settlements possess at least one Public House, but in recent times with the recession and austerity many have sadly been forced to call last orders for the final time. Bradshaw is no exception as I found the old

Beer House named the Bradshaw Tavern boarded up. Luckily the Golden Fleece with its live football courtesy of the great God Sky still serves up finely brewed local ales so all is not lost.

A Beerhouse was a type of drinking establishment created by the 1830 Beerhouse Act. Legally defined as a place "where beer is sold to be consumed on the premises", just about anyone could brew their own beer, open up their front room and sell to anyone they wanted. The intention was to increase competition between brewers, and it resulted in the opening of hundreds of new Beerhouses, public houses and breweries throughout the country, particularly in the rapidly expanding industrial centres of the north of England.

Public houses at the time were issued with licenses by local magistrates under the terms of the Retail Brewers Act 1828, and were subject to police inspections at any time of the day or night. The proprietors of Beerhouses on the other hand simply had to buy a license from the government costing two guineas per annum, equivalent to about £150 as of 2010. Until the Wine and Beerhouse Act of 1869 gave local magistrates the authority to renew Beerhouse licenses, the two classes of establishment were in direct competition.

The Act's supporters hoped that by increasing competition in the brewing and sale of beer, and thus lowering its price, the population might be weaned off more alcoholic drinks such as gin. But it proved to be controversial, removing as it did the monopoly of local magistrates to lucratively regulate local trade in alcohol, and not applying retrospectively to those who already ran public houses. It was also denounced as promoting drunkenness.

There was a time in the history of Bradshaw when the population was much larger than it is today. A large number of wool combers, spinners, and weavers occupied cottages in the village or on the hillsides, and work was brought in from Brookhouse and other places nearby. But the introduction of machinery, and the application of steam effected a great change.

Bradshaw mill was opened in 1855 to provide employment for the villagers after local coal mines had closed down. This large mill stood six storeys high and was constructed on land donated by John Lassey. Owners and tenants of the mill have included Pickles, Whitley & Midgley (1861), Patchett & Company, H. & B. Broadbent of Cleckheaton and T. S. Tetley Limited (1905).

It was finally taken over by Lister's of Manningham Mills, Bradford before being closed in 1967. Today only the mill pond remains and the site contains modern housing.

As Lou Parson and I travelled on through the village the source of the laughing and screaming children's voices that I had heard way back at Raggalds became apparent. It was lunchtime at the village school and the yard was rammed with young boys running around, playing football and play fighting. The girls stood around just chatting and doing nothing. Walking off laughing, the concept of such things being ingrained even at such a young age was not lost on me.

I was feeling more than a little giddy as I reached the village War Memorial and the church of St. John's as I knew that a short distance away stood wide open pastures and the comforting aroma of some of the regions finest countryside. It was within this kind of landscape that I always enjoyed a feeling of calm and relaxation and every historical walk that I have ever done has contained something of this type of land.

The life-giving ball of fire in the sky which we call the Sun took this opportunity to break free from behind the clouds. Its power and strength compelled me to remove my well trusted black flat cap and allow its rays to warm my rapidly balding head. The comforting mooing of cows in the middle distance seemed to draw me along School Lane like a sailing ship being entrapped by a Siren. The man washing his car outside Scausby Hall took a break from his task to bid Lou and I a pleasant greeting.

All was well on planet Jackson and the rapidly advancing smell of the open fields only served to enhance this feeling. Summer breeze makes me feel fine, blowing through the Jasmin in my mind. Ok so it was not yet summer but that great tune wafted around my head as I strode on along School Lane.

Not for the first time I had to consult my Smartphone map of the area as I was looking for a tiny footpath that would take Lou and I through an area marked as Rifle Range and on towards Strines Beck. I duly found the footpath tucked along in front of a tiny row of cottages that enjoys the evocative name of "St. John's Cross". After perhaps one hundred feet I was making good progress across the rifle range and towards an area known as The Gulf and beyond that the rising edifice of Royd Hill.

Strines Beck itself forms the boundary between Bradford and Halifax and usually burbles along at quite a rate and more so today due to the recent rainy weather. Here I crossed over the beck by way of an ancient stone footbridge and started the lung-bursting climb up the hill towards Royd Hill.

This area below Roper Lane is a south and west facing hillside of conifers, alders, rowan, and holly. The word Royd denotes a clearing in a forest and the large house of Oats Royd stands in just such a place.

The hillside above the house, known as "The Gulf" holds large numbers of birds such as Willow Warbler, continental Robins on passage and also Flycatcher, Redstart, Whitethroat and Whinchat. The conifers above the house hold Tawny owl and smaller owls can always be picked out on the walls around the bottom fields. The holly bushes attract winter thrushes and Green Woodpeckers, the latter being a resident breeder.

Down near the beck, Siskins use the Alder trees and Wrens nest in the bankings, and the four man-made ponds at the bottom are home to resident breeding Coot, Moorhen and Mallard along with occasional Canada Goose. Add to this the presence of Kestrels up on the thermals above the Gulf, Roe Deer and Fox down below and you have a most wonderful nature sanctuary. As I started the long steep climb to the top I looked down at Lou and stated out loud that a place like this must be preserved as a monument to nature at all costs. The sun had clearly gone to my head so back on went the black flat cap.

Reaching the summit I could clearly see one of the capped off air shafts for the magnificent railway tunnel that runs from the far side of Queensbury and ends at Strines cutting. The large circular stone structure stands only four feet above ground level and I could not resist jumping on top to survey the land below. The in filled cutting way down below is still visible although today it is surrounded by an ever encroaching industrial estate.

Connecting Holmfield station to Queensbury involved two large constructions with the firm of Benton and Woodiwiss being employed as the contractors. Strines Cutting was 1,033 yards long and 59 feet deep and took several years to provide with adequate drainage. Queensbury tunnel is 2,501 yards long and 430 feet beneath ground level at its deepest and took four years to complete.

The tunnel contains 5 ventilation shafts ranging from 112ft to 379ft and 8 construction shafts were used in the construction. Much of the work was done by blasting. At the time of its completion the tunnel was the longest on the GNR and such was the height difference between Holmfield and Queensbury stations that the tunnel was on a continuous gradient of 1 in 100 (1% grade) falling towards Holmfield.

Ten workers were killed during the construction of the tunnel, one when a metal cage used in one of the construction shafts was overwound at the top of the shaft, breaking the rope. The cage fell to the bottom of the shaft, through the wooden doors and landed on three workers, killing one. His father was also working in the tunnel. (To put that in context twenty-two men were killed during the construction of the Bramhope tunnel north of Leeds).

Being so deep the tunnel had its own problems. Many locos were damaged by huge icicles forming on the roof of the tunnel. Engines were sometimes left running in the tunnel to prevent their formation. Sometimes, smoke and steam would linger so densely in the tunnel that drivers failed to realise they were nearing the end of the tunnel at Queensbury station.

To alert them to this a huge gong was installed, the arm of which was struck by the front of the train. Amazingly the remnants of this fitting are still there in the tunnel. With the completed construction of the line between Holmfield and Queensbury the whole section from Bradford to Halifax was opened for goods traffic on 1 December 1879 and for passenger trains two weeks later.

I quickly reached Roper Lane, and after crossing made my way along Ladysmith Road past tight quaint old cottages that lined the thin street. Looking up my eyes picked out a fast approaching figure in the distance. I was not unduly concerned with the man as my gaze was attracted to the tiny dog that trotted dutifully along at his heels. A large smile worked its way across my face as the small but perfectly formed Jack Russell came into focus.

Even at a distance I could tell the dog was a female by its gait and the swagger of its back end. Just like humans the Jack Russell has different back ends for both male and female. I quickened my step to close the distance between us and within seconds this most appealing little dog and Lou Parson were checking each other out in that peculiar canine way.

Lou Parson does not tolerate male dogs of any variety, but with females she occasionally has no problems at all. The stranger and I stood there observing this meeting of the breed and he seemed as engrossed in the proceedings as I was. There were no ill feelings of any sort between these two fine dogs and after they had said their hello's they both stood motionless as the stranger and I chewed the fat so to speak for a couple of minutes. We swapped tales of our previous Jacks, lamenting past little canine friends before parting and going our separate ways.

As simple as it sounds this all too brief interlude was the highlight of the day for both Lou and myself. Such occasions are sadly all too rare and it made the final mile-long walk back to base at Sand Beds a breeze.

Thanks old man I hope we will meet again sometime on our travels around the Queensbury area.

Walking in the Shadow of the Fosters

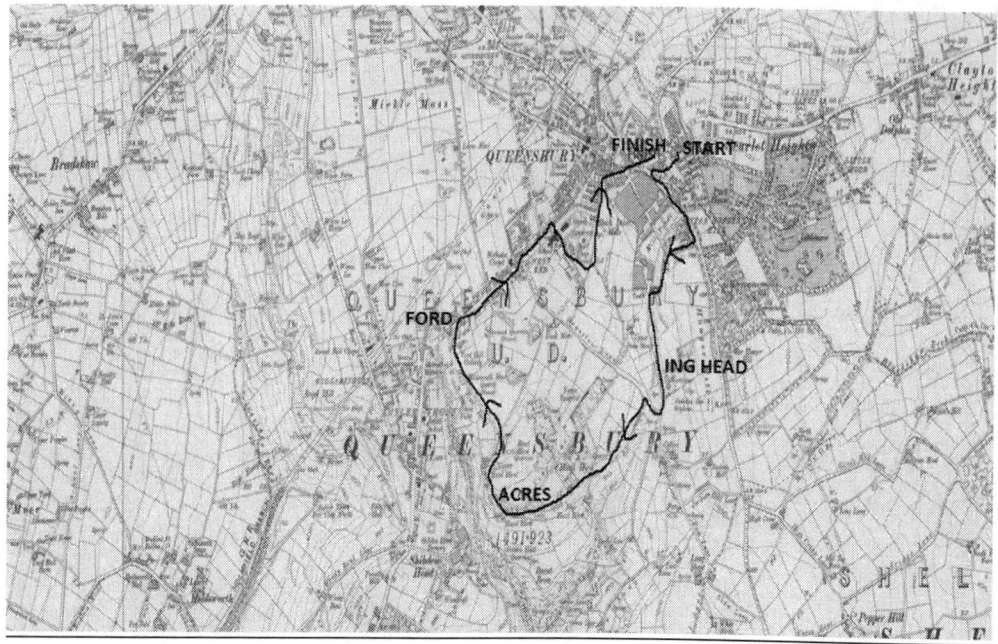

Sometimes the historical walks that Lou Parson and I do are planned with meticulous detail more deserving of a military campaign. Sometimes they are more a spur of the moment thing. This trot around Queensbury was one of those occasions when the idea simply dropped into my head and that was enough to get me speeding off in a different gear.

The afternoon in late January was dry and bright as Lou Parson and I set off from our base at Brickfields. My intention was to view some of the properties and buildings constructed and financed by the Foster family, and of course there are many in and around the village. So with this in mind I surfaced on the old Leeds and Halifax Turnpike Trust road at Sand Beds but to avoid confusion I will use its present day name of the A647.

Here by the Cottage Stores the road is always busy with passing traffic and it took what seemed like an age for the crossing to stem the traffic and allow Lou and I access to the magnificent Grade II listed Victoria Hall on the far side. Built by Foster's own workforce from 1888-1891 to commemorate Queen Victoria's Golden Jubilee, Victoria Hall was designed by the Bradford firm of T.H. and F Healy in the "Queen Anne revival" style of architecture.

In British architecture the term is mostly used in relation to domestic buildings up to the size of a manor house, and usually designed elegantly but simply by local builders or architects, rather than the grand palaces of noble magnates.

The Public hall incorporates a library and council chamber plus a later addition of an extension housing a small swimming bath. Sadly the Library will close permanently on 29th March 2017 (shame on you Bradford Council) The 1891 Ordnance Survey map of Queensbury suggests that there was also a formal garden or park planted behind the Hall, but today that area is covered by a car park and a little further away a private dwelling.

Lou always gets a little excited when I allow her to scratch in the flower beds at the front as she knows there are Chickens in the private garden just over the wall. This belongs to Edward House which is the first of three smart villas which were also built around this time by the Foster family for their mill managers. The adjacent villas are named Albert House and Highfield. The Foster influence continues with the next group of buildings with the former carriage house and stables which stand next door to the former Stag's Head Inn (I prefer this name rather than any of the number of subsequent titles given to this ancient building).

This is where the waggons and horses that were used to transport the wool and finished goods from Black Dyke Mills were kept. This building also housed the Mill's fire brigade. Its former equestrian use is reflected in the enclosed courtyard and single storey stable blocks, now used as a barber's shop and garages. The main building features an elliptical arched main carriage entrance with wood-panelled doors, round-headed windows and a central pediment with an oculus. The three decorative ventilators on the stone slate roof are most distinctive. Today this building is in something of a poor state of repair but the recent appearance of scaffolding does bode well for the future in respect of renovation work.

I annoyed the passing traffic once again by activating the crossing at the lights. The bloke in the Range Rover shot me a look like I had just robbed his house and shot his cat, but in a few seconds we were gone and his life could carry on once again. Here at the junction stands another of John Foster's buildings. It is quite an important building as Prospect House and the adjacent warehouse was the base from where John Foster's business empire began.

Built in 1827 Prospect House is separated from the main road by a low wall with iron railings. These stand on either side of a large square stone porch which was previously linked to the main building by glazing. The fixing points for the glass panels can still be seen on the stone walls. Apart from this, very little distinguishes this building architecturally from others in the village centre although the front door has a semi-circular transom above it and its two multi-flue chimneys with tall clay pots are unique in the village. The warehouse behind has blocked loading bays at first-floor level and was used as a billiard room and workshop before it became to be used as an office.

As I stood on the junction I was glad that I had no intention of yet again crossing this busy and congested junction. From this side the majestic three-storey warehouse of Black Dyke Mills and the Albert fountain can clearly be seen. The warehouse was the building where customers could see samples of the yarn and cloth produced at the mill, and like the rest of the mill, this Grade II listed building features hammer-dressed stone but it is broken up by ashlar stone dressings in the form of stringcourses and window reveals. The three central bays project forward and are framed by pilasters which are beneath a simpler entablature on top of which stands an openwork parapet with four large finials on top of its cornice which give the warehouse a crown-like centrepiece, especially as the roof is not visible.

The Albert Memorial Fountain stands on a four step plinth in front of the warehouse and is also Grade II listed. It was built on behalf of the Fosters and opened in 1863 to the design of E Milnes and C France, who designed many of the mill buildings in Little Germany in Bradford. It is gothic in style and made from carved ashlar stone apart from the troughs, which are made from red granite. Above the trough are four allegorical figures representing Agriculture, Industry, Literature and Fine Art. Four pinnacles are carved to resemble foliage and surround an octagonal stage on which stands an octagonal cross-topped spire supported by eight colonnades. It is one of the few outwardly gothic and intricately crafted structures in the conservation area and is even more unusual in its use of stone from elsewhere.

Influence of the Foster family still pervades almost every aspect of the village of Queensbury. Even today their mark can be seen in the physical sense by way of the multitude of buildings they financed and sanctioned, and equally so by the tales of history their presence has left upon the very fabric of the village.

Walking along the main road out towards Hunger Hill, this notion became even more apparent as I passed the site of the former Gasworks. Again constructed and financed by the Foster family to provide the fledgeling technology to the village, the site is now occupied by the large Tesco supermarket. A little further beyond was Foster's brickworks to which the present day estate of former mill workers dwellings takes its name.

The main road is flanked on the other side by the two storey former mechanics' shop and counting house of Foster's Black Dyke Mill. Built into the hillside, this small-scale building extends over the former yard entrance with its façade onto Brighouse Road broken into three sections. The central section houses the now bricked up and sealed segmental archway, which led into the yard. The carved eaves and triangular pediment break up the otherwise nondescript frontage and draws attention to the gateway. Black Dyke Mill workers donated the clock face that sits within the pediment to John Foster in 1848 in gratitude for steady and regular employment at a time when the industry as a whole was prone to volatile fluctuation in the numbers of people it employed. On the rooftop, above the pinnacle of the pediment, there is a small octagonal cupola, which houses a bell and has an iron weather vane at its apex.

Although I had walked but a short distance I was looking forward to breaking out into open pasture. For it is here that Lou Parson comes into her own and I take great delight in watching her darting about and following trails as we amble along. As I turned off the main road along Vale Grove I knew there was a tiny old footpath at the end which would take us out into the space that I so craved. Here on the right of Vale Grove stands another fine example of the type of villas constructed by the Foster family in which to house their mill managers.

The footpath can be found at the end of this previously cobbled road. It leads around the rear of the 1930's houses of Medway and Ridgeway and onto an expanse of open pasture. Here I allowed the leash out to its maximum extent and Lou took full advantage to stretch her finely sculptured legs for the first time.

The area Lou and I were trekking through is marked on the old Ordnance Survey maps as Ing Head. Ings is an old word of Norse origin referring to water meadows and marshes and that I could believe as the ground was wet and spongy in the extreme.

After a short struggle I emerged from the watery morass at the junction of Deanstones Lane, Green Lane and Syke Lane, and from here proceeded along another small footpath which runs along the crest of the small valley leading to Green Lane quarry. After only a few yards I stopped and focused my gaze upon the larger and slightly distant head of Shibden Valley. I was not heading down that way today but oh yes it was certainly on my "to do list" in the near future.

The footpath quickly led me to an area of what I would term "open moorland", although not quite open in the sense of Ilkley Moor it is still a substantial area. Away to the right beyond the school playing pitches stands Long Lane where modern day housing stands on the former site of the Isolation or "Fever" hospital.

The isolation hospital was built in the days when infectious diseases were still a major medical problem. On 24th June, 1882, a deputation was sent to meet John Foster to enquire about the possibility of purchasing a field in Long Lane for such a hospital, but it was unsuccessful. In April, 1893, however, the same people agreed to buy land from George Ambler for £280 and a hospital with twenty beds was built by the Local Board and opened the same year. The Central block housed the Matron and local GPs provided medical cover.

In the first ten years there had been 251 patients: 249 cases of Scarlet Fever, one of Diphtheria and one of Enteric Fever. Four cases of Scarlet Fever died. Unfortunately no record exists of the total number of patients treated in the hospitals fifty-two years of existence. Since the advent of Sulphonamides in 1937 and Penicillin in 1942 and the subsequent inoculation program, the Hospital was closed in 1945. Patients who needed isolation were sent to Bradford Isolation Hospital on Leeds Road. Locals remember being taken to the hospital in a horse-drawn ambulance, the left of the building being for diphtheria patients and the right for scarlet fever sufferers.

Lou Parson and I continued along the footpath admiring the vista across the valley towards Bare head Quarry as we went. The whole of the valley below us is pockmarked with signs of previous industrial use, some at Bare Head that I had seen on a previous visit and some a little further down the valley which I would soon be investigating on a future historical walk.

The footpath led me past pockets of heather above the house named Near Hazel Hirst before depositing me via a rickety old gate near to Lower Hazel Hirst in an area named "Acres". All these Hazel's and Hirst's it was becoming quite confusing and we were not finished yet as there was another one to come shortly.

As my intrepid Jack Russell partner in crime pulled me onto Long Lane I was taken aback by the sheer size and scale of the vast spoil retaining wall for the former Sandstone quarry above. I was surprised not so much by the scale of the wall but more by the fact that its presence was totally unexpected. These substantial constructions are known as "Judd Ramparts", and this dry stone wall built with not even the slightest amount of mortar dominates this section of Long Lane. The green tinged stones have not moved an inch since the day they were laid over a century ago.

As I walked along Long lane I became engrossed in the intoxicating sight of this huge creation. So much so that I failed to notice the pothole looming up in front of me. Down into the hole went my left foot and over my ankle buckled. The expletive I shot out must surely have been heard all the way down the Shibden Valley.

It was the same ankle that I had injured on a slippy Roman road on Blackstone Edge moor three months previously, but happily the pain was nothing like as severe this second time. The only course to take was to continue and walk it off so with this in mind I hobbled away towards Ford like an old man coming out of the Halfway House after twelve pints. I was in so much pain I hardly noticed the ancient dwelling of Upper Hazel Hirst as I passed.

By the time I had managed to drag my aching foot along to the former site of Ford Hill Colliery, I felt like I had marched through the Burma jungle in six-inch Stiletto heels. Today the area consists of a council recycling centre and household refuse tip but many years ago it was the site of a small coal pit.

The mine was operational from 1897 when the first shaft was sunk and was worked until 1941 when production ended. In 1918 the mine was owned by M Stocks and the Underground Manager was Charles Brown. The pit was listed as having forty underground workers and six surface workers registered. Ford Hill Colliery was only one of many such small coal pits in the Queensbury area and by the 1920's the workings had branched out some seven hundred yards in search of the soft bed coal.

It had been my intention to simply stroll like an Edwardian playboy along Fleet Lane to Foxhill then turn back along Albert road to base at Sandbeds, but my ankle was now throbbing like a drunk driver's heart as he spots a Police car in his rear view mirror so I turned up Ford Hill and headed for home. Lou Parson was well aware that all was not well as she understood my mumbled cursing and swearing as we plodded along the pavement, and made things a little easier by trotting along at my side rather than her usual "I lead the way you human follow me" brand of pulling.

The area named Swamp, West End and the cemetery came and went with me hardly noticing and it was with more than a sense of relief that I made it to the High Street. My big idea to walk off the pain had not worked and matters were made even worse by my occasional attack of Gout deciding to join the party. Hobbling down the street like a demented old crab I was in a right mess. It was a good job I was fairly new to the village and no one really knew me as I drew stares and disapproving looks aplenty.

The traffic lights by the Albert fountain had never looked so bright and welcoming, and the bath that night had never felt so good.

A Brewery and a Beck

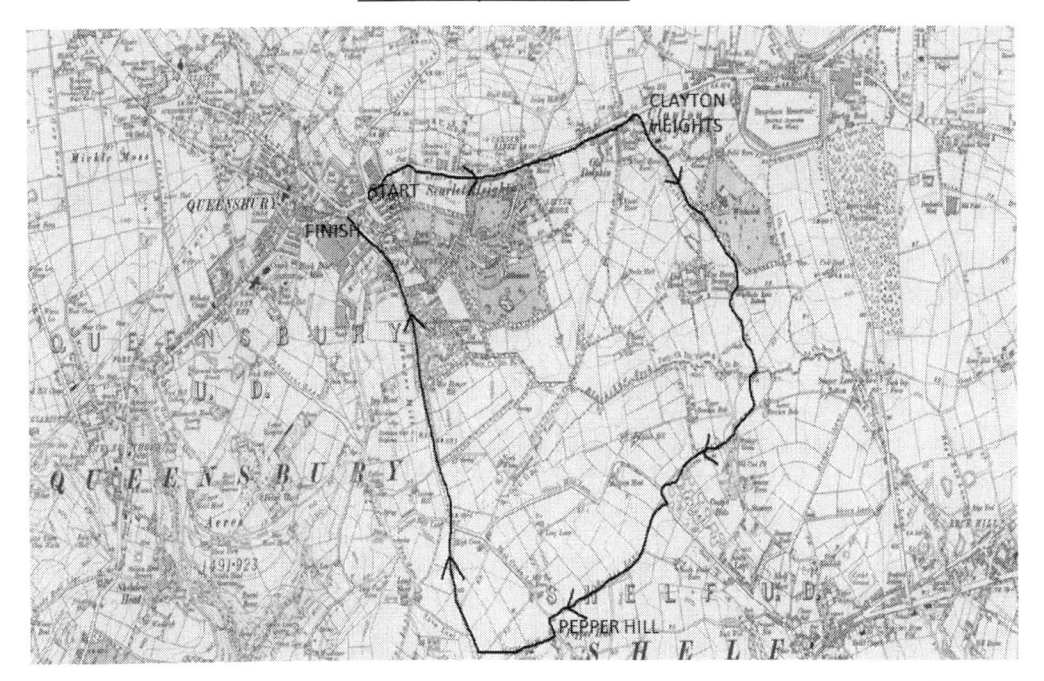

Whilst I am in no way a religious man I do have something of an interest in the architecture of religious buildings. They may be simple or grand but I just have an admiration for some of the edifices that the Church have created over the years. Most of all I admire the tiny out of the way simple places of worship where simple people would go to do their thing so to speak.

The motivation for this historical walk was the discovery on an old Ordnance Survey map of just such a place at Pepper Hill near Shelf. Surrounded by isolated farms and cottages the congregation must surely have been tiny and this intrigued me enough to scan the area and see what else I could come up with.

Thursday the nineteenth of January was the first day for a while that had promised to be rain free. After checking the weather forecast, the intrepid Lou Parson and I set sail once again along the main road from Sandbeds to Clayton Heights. The Leeds and Halifax Turnpike Trust to use the original name, is a busy stretch of road that had become very familiar to me as I had started to use it to access the start of quite a few of my walks around the Queensbury area. It only took me five minutes or so to leave Sandbeds behind and get to the spot overlooking the railway triangle. I always stop here to admire the view down the valley and across to Thornton.

Surely this must have been the place where the Victorian Surveyors and Engineers stood when they were planning the railways in the valley below them all those years ago?

Stopping as I approached the fine row of roadside cottages named Calderbanks, I paused for a moment to admire the superb residential house called Winterbank. I was told that this house with its superb views across upper Bradford-dale was built by the Foster family to accommodate male workers at the nearby Black Dyke Mill in Queensbury. Judging by its stature I would say it housed men of "manager" status like the houses next to the Victoria Hall at Sand Beds rather than the lower ranked mill workers.

Passing quickly by the entrance to Littlemoor Park, Lou and I were soon at The Old Dolphin Inn. This former "baiting House" for the Stagecoaches of the time was a popular stopping over point for travellers heading towards the Cotton city of Manchester. The large adjoining stable complex had room for thirty horses and that was a sign of its popularity. As Lou and I moved off from outside the pub I had to cross the road due to the two large German Shepherds and their owner closing on us quickly. The owner appeared to be struggling somewhat to control the dogs so this was the best course of action. I was going to do this anyway as I wanted to have a quick view into the three tiny squares that sneaked away behind the roadside cottages. Patchett Square is the most appealing with its cobbled entrance leading into something of a time bubble. The tiny cottages huddled together spoke volumes about the way the local quarrymen, farmers and coal workers lived in the late eighteenth century.

A little further on by the junction with Stocks Lane stands Clayton Heights war memorial. Like most other village memorials to the war dead it is simple and unobtrusive in design which in itself lends an air of dignity which is not found in the larger and grander versions. It consists of a Latin cross with a column set on a curved bottomed plinth with garland decorated cap and dedication. The memorial stands on a platform with brick built sides and contains the names of eighteen men who died in WW1 and six who died in WW2.

Stocks Lane would take Lou and I out into the countryside for the first time today. The iron gates and ornate posts of Springfield House gave way to mature trees that lined the lane on one side to give me an indication of the presence of the grounds of the former Westwood Hall.

Looking back towards Queensbury it felt most strange to not see the usual spectre of Foster's great mill chimney observing me like a stern 1950's Policeman. It was to become one of the few places where Fosters finest erection could not be seen as I have used it as a guiding point more than once as I rambled around the area.

The grounds of the former Westwood Hall are today crammed with modern new build houses which hold no attraction for me. Perhaps one of its former owners who built the house in 1861, Lt. Cot. Henry Sagar Hirst would not approve either. Another previous owner who turned the hall into a hospital, Bradford Council, certainly would approve but progress is not always good. These new carbuncles melted away behind more mature trees as I reached the end of Stocks Lane. Here the track split into two with one track leading to the stone entrance gateposts of Low House and the other leading into a small wooded area.

Low House and the subsequent Brewery was owned for generations by members of the prominent Claytonian Hirst family. John Hirst bought Low House in 1665 from the trustees of his father in law, Abraham Brathwaite. The house was then known as Brightwater. Yarn was spun for a while on hand looms on premises adjoining Low House. At the age of 21, Henry Sagar joined his elder brother Joseph, who had started a brewing business at Low House and from 1851 they traded as Messrs J & H.S.Hirst. Sometime after that Joseph Hirst and Henry Sagar Hirst formed Low House Brewery and subsequently named it The Lion Brewery. Joseph died in 1890 and in 1893 his Sons sold the whole estate to Bentleys Breweries. Today, what remains of the house is in private hands and due to the racket that a number of seemingly large dogs were making I decided that I would backtrack to the fork in the track and go through the small wooded area.

This wooded area gave way to a large grass covered mound of earth that was lined on one side by a quaint Cricket pitch. Here was the site of a long gone farmhouse named Stocks Lane Bottom. I made a mental note to spend a summer Saturday afternoon watching local Cricket here in the near future.

Now at last Lou Parson and I were in open countryside, and after the mildly oppressive nature of the mature trees and woodland behind us, I found I could once again breathe deeply in a sense and it was a feeling that I welcomed.

The ground beneath my feet was sodden due to the nearby springs and the recent rainfall. I was not concerned as I knew that nearby Blackshaw Beck would be full and fast flowing and a beck in full cry is a joy to behold. Upon arriving at the beck I found it to be indeed swollen and settling on a large rock I wistfully wasted away a few minutes simply admiring the cold water as it made its unstoppable way across the field. Crossing the beck by an ancient stone sided footbridge, I headed across the sodden fields once again making for the famous but strangely odd Lion Gate.

This structure once formed the Southern entrance to the Low House estate and stands at the point where Stanage Lane becomes Brackens Lane. This structure consists of a large square stone gateway with a resting stone Lion perched upon the top flanked by two smaller pedestrian gates.

The features of the Lion are heavily weathered due to Mother Nature and the passing of time. To each side of the gate are the smaller arched gateways but sadly all three entrances were locked and chained. I had visited this area previously during a walk for my first book and I remembered that I was not far from the site of the last working Windmill in the Shelf district. So a short detour was in order as it would have been rude to have not revisited the site on Burned Road.

This windmill was used to grind locally grown corn and was the last in the district to survive. Before falling into disrepair it remained as a local landmark until in 1960 when the top of the building was destroyed by a lightning strike before being finally demolished in 1964. Each of the four sails was seven feet in width and sixty feet in length and weighed one tonne. In 1904, the sails were removed and a stream engine was introduced to provide power to grind the corn from the local farms. In 1914, the owner at the time Francis Barraclough closed the business and it remained unused until its final demise.

The actual site of the Windmill is now simply a piece of scrub land behind the remaining cottage. Standing there I used my imagination to conjure up images of the massive lofty sails thundering through the air as they whirled through their repetitive windy dance. I was abruptly jerked from my daydream by the honking of a passing car horn.

"Too much time on your hand's mate, get a job".

He had rounded the corner and was out of sight before I managed to give him the traditional working man's salute.

Backtracking along Stanage Lane, I once again passed the Lion Gate as I strode along Brackens Lane. Half way along this peaceful lane is a walled off track that leads back into the former estate for Low House. This was the access track for the long gone hamlet of Upper Bracken Beds. This tiny settlement was recorded as having being built in the early eighteenth century possibly by Ayton and Elwell the bridge builders and founders, for their workers. Today only a small number of bumps and humps in the ground remain as evidence of this small hamlet.

Across the road the pasture on the left is pockmarked with a number of former tiny coal pits and the area deserves the name "Coal Pit Hills". The ground on this small area dips and undulates as a result of the settling of the infill of the pits which were known as Bell Pits.

A bell pit is a primitive method of mining coal, iron ore or other minerals where the coal or ore lies near the surface. A shaft is sunk to reach the mineral which is excavated by miners, transported to the surface by a winch, and removed by means of a bucket, much like a well. It gets its name because the pit in cross section resembles a bell. Typically, no supports were used and mining continued outwards until the cavity became too dangerous or collapsed at which point another mine was started, often in close proximity. This type of mine was in use in prehistoric times and the Middle Ages.

Such pits are common at prehistoric flint-working sites such as Grime's Graves in Norfolk and also in the coal mining areas of Yorkshire, the Forest of Dean, and Leicestershire. Bell pits often flooded due to a lack of a drainage system. This, together with the lack of support and the likelihood of collapse, meant they had a limited lifespan. Bell pits were not very effective for mining as they only partially exploited the resources. The remains of bell pits can sometimes be identified by depressions left when they collapsed and it is these depressions that can be seen today on Coal Pit Hills.

Upon checking my map I discovered that I had to take Bridge Lane and cross half a mile of the muddiest and most heavily fly tipped terrain that I had yet seen during my Queensbury walks. Pile after pile of general house and building detritus made me shake my head more times than a man at a Motorhead concert as I trudged along through the mud.

What motivates these people to scar and defile such beautiful landscape was the question that I asked myself as I struggled along to hopefully better views at Pepper Hill.

Pepper hill is no more than a tiny hamlet consisting of a clutch of early nineteenth century cottages, a farm or two and of course the Chapel. The farmyard of Pepper Hill Farm appears to be a facility for the wintering of caravans as well as a working farm. Only one hundred yards or so further along is the marvellous Unitarian Chapel that I had spied the night before on the Ordnance Survey map.

The historic Unitarian affirmation "God is One" is the notion that gave the movement its name. Today, this stress on divine unity has broadened. Now Unitarians also affirm: Humanity is one, the World is one, the Interdependent Web of Life is one. But while Unitarians may share these affirmations, they do so in an open and liberal spirit. So it's a bit like Amsterdam then I guess?

In the year 1858 Mr. A Stradling, a working man who had recently joined the Northgate End congregation at Halifax, possessed with a convert's zeal, was anxious to do something for the cause he had espoused. He began visiting the neglected hamlet of Pepper Hill, and founded, first, a Mutual Improvement Society, and then a Sunday school. For their place of meeting a cottage was hired and the rent paid by the members, and when evening service was commenced, there was often a crowd of sixty or seventy persons in the little room.

In 1862 the present building was opened, and, though intended for public worship, the original name "School-House" was maintained. The trust deed provides that the building shall be "used for the assembling of a congregation for the worship of Almighty God, and for schools and classes for religious and general improvement and instruction, and for lectures and other means of social improvement. Since 1904 the chapel has seen mixed fortunes with near disaster when the roof collapsed completely in the 1930's

In more modern times the Chapel has undergone major improvement with the fitting of a new internal disabled toilet, a disabled ramp, a hot air heating system and has been fully redecorated. The chapel has the highest Unitarian pulpit in England and is said to be 1005 feet above sea level.

Pepper Hill Chapel has the dubious honour of once been frequented by the man who broke the bank at Monte Carlo. Joseph Hobson Jagger was an engineer at Bottomley's Mill in Shelf and in the 1870's he went to Monte Carlo to visit the casinos. Using his engineering skills he studied the Roulette wheels and devised a method with which to beat it. On July 7th, 1875 he placed his first bet and eight days later he had won two million old French Francs. This would be the equivalent of £400,000 today which in the 1870's was a huge sum of money. His secret method to beat the system was all to do with the cylinders of the Roulette wheel apparently.

I tip my hat to anyone who takes on "the system" and beats it. Jagger is buried in the graveyard of the Independent Methodist Chapel named The Bethel Chapel on Carr House Road in Shelf.

Some years ago a member of the congregation at Pepper Hill was married in the chapel and along with other personalities amongst the invited guests was Sir Paul and Linda McCartney. Unfortunately on the day the couple was unable to attend due to ill health on the part of Mrs. McCartney and the potential inspiration for another of Sir Paul's songs went begging.

Across the country lane from the Chapel is a kind of a stone seat set into the dry stone wall. Here I plonked my weary bones down and opened up my tobacco tin and started to roll a smoke. This was the first occasion that I had rested since I left home and it was welcome as the mud and sodden fields had made me feel like I had been walking for three weeks. As the Nicotine started to soothe my body I looked across the road at the tiny beguiling Chapel in the middle of nowhere.

My imagination started to stir and I found myself conjuring up mental images of a large crowd of screaming young girls surrounding a white Bentley as it disgorged Mr and Mrs McCartney into the tight country lane. Flanked by security guards the couple struggled to pass through the crowd and it was only the intervention of Father McKenzie that enabled them to enter the safety of the Chapel. I bet it made a change from writing the words to a sermon that no one will hear.

As the roll up burned its way down to my fingers I decided it was time for this day tripper to depart for home. So I let it be and started down the long and winding road back towards Sand Beds and a welcome and yet another well-deserved hot bath.

Shibden dale and Black Boy House

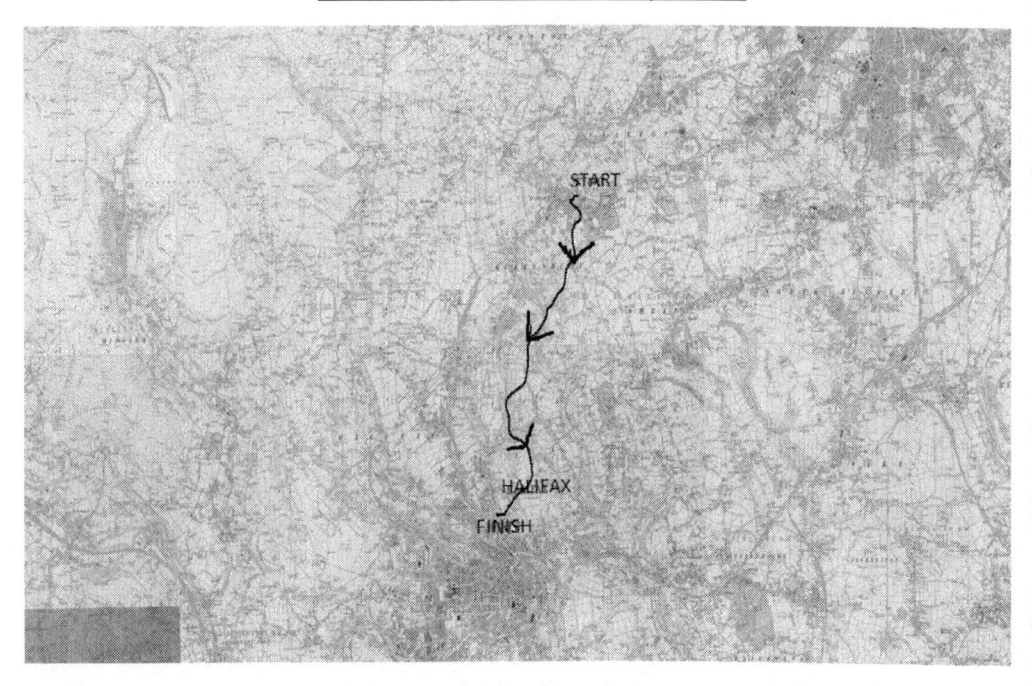

Wednesday 15th of March dawned with the promised sunshine already cracking the flags as I rose and opened up the bedroom curtains. I had a new pair of walking boots that needed to be broken in so the long-planned trip down the Shibden Valley seemed like a great idea. This walk was originally planned as part of my historical walking book based on Calderdale but when I decided to halt work on that book and concentrate on the Queensbury area I brought this walk back to life so to speak. The original starting point was always going to be from the main road at Ford but at the last minute I changed things around and decided to enter Shibden Dale from Green Lane near Ing Head instead.

After sorting things out at home Lou Parson and I set off along the Brighouse and Denholme Road towards Hunger Hill. Turning up Vale Grove and passing the mill managers houses again, I soon found myself being dragged along at speed across the pasture towards the site of John Foster's original mill. Marked on the old OS maps as "Warehouse" it was initially a worsted mill that predates the later mill a little further up at Black Dyke by a number of years.

This area off the end of Deanstones Lane is named Ings Head which means "water meadow" and it deserves its name as the pasture was spongy and waterlogged as my new walking boots got their first test.

As I crossed the field I looked ahead and the compound where the mill once stood could clearly be seen. Piles of proud Yorkshire stone stood silent and forgotten until the time when they will be reused for another building. But with the image of a photo of the mill set in my mind it was easy to imagine how the mill must have looked. The mill was constructed on land that had been in John Foster's wife's family since 1779 and at four to five stories high it dominated the area until the construction of Foster's new mill nearby took over the mantel.

Once Foster had moved his operation to the new much larger mill this mill became a hostel for young women and girls who had travelled from far and wide to take up offers of employment in the Worsted trade. They came from Italy and Malta as well as the North East of England as there had been an increasing difficulty in finding sufficient spinners in the village of Queensbury. The directors hit upon the excellent plan of providing accommodation in the well-equipped hostel. This hostel contained 231 beds, a large dining room, comfortably furnished public rooms, and a kitchen fitted up with all modern conveniences. At one end of the mill there stood a small row of three cottages with the end dwelling being adapted into a small shop that sold snacks and bits and bobs to the young girls at the hostel.

I understand the building was demolished in the mid-1970's and today apart from the piles of stones very little remains. I had to launch Lou Parson over a wall that had a ten-foot drop on the other side, and when I finished struggling over it myself I wondered if it had been built at such a height to keep the girls in the hostel or the randy village boys out.

The sun had warmed up well as Lou propelled us along Green Lane towards the site of another disappeared building. This time it was a small cottage named Green Lane Top that once stood at the entrance to an ancient footpath leading down into the hidden and mystical head of Shibden Dale. After plodding across another sodden field then through a convenient opening in a huge Holly bush, the valley opened up before me. I estimated the drop down the steep side to be fifty feet or so and I could hear the rushing stream on the floor so I had something to aim for as I slowly picked my way down through the vegetation.

The stream at this point actually starts as a spring that pours out of the rocks half way down the valley side. Further down the valley it joins with Shibden Brook which itself starts as another spring over near my original starting point at Ford. The house of Near Hazel Hirst on the far upper slopes of the valley disappeared from view as I slowly inched my way down through the mixed vegetation. Lou parson of course was steaming headlong down towards the valley floor and it took all my strength and composure to just keep steady and not go crashing down into the flowing water.

But the hard work was worth it when I eventually reached the bottom. The spring had become a stream but not yet a beck as it weaved its way past moss covered fallen tree trunks. Cutting a channel through the thin soil on the floor the amazingly clear water paid us no notice as it flowed relentlessly on southwards. A huge bed of spring Bluebells blocked my path and Lou was intent on pulling me right through the centre, but I wasn't having any of that and stepping aside like George Best fooling the most competent defence, I tested my new boots even further as I skipped through the water.

Down in this mystical and timeless place there was no sign of any modern day rubbish or detritus. Yes there was the odd tyre dotted around in the water but these had been here that long they were now completely covered in green moss and simply blended in with the natural surroundings. There were no Coke cans, fag packets or biscuit wrappers for a change and I felt like I was the first person to ever come here.

As steep and as narrow as this small valley was there was no feeling of oppression or containment. The available light was good and the air was quiet and time just seemed to stand still as the Jack Russell and I made our way towards a series of flat rocks that form an ancient ford at Henacre Wood. Although it had only taken perhaps twenty minutes to reach this point it seemed like an hour due to the fallen trees and branches making the going difficult. Here at the ford the water from Shibden Brook joins and together they form a greater flowing body of water. The many tiny springs that emanate from the steep rocks along the edge also contribute to the velocity of the water as it leaves the quietness of the ford and continues on towards Halifax.

As I wandered along I noticed a simple footpath leading up the valley side to a pasture near to Hanging Royd. Lou scampered up leaving me struggling breathlessly behind but after only a few seconds we had both reached the field above.

Here people had been wild camping as the tell-tale signs of rudimentary campfires lay all around. I made a mental note to remember this spot for the summer if I too get the urge to sleep under canvas.

By now I had allowed Lou Parson to dictate the route as I occasionally do and this she did with her usual enthusiasm. She decided to re-join the footpath as it wound its way along the centre of the rapidly widening valley and led me to a bankside area dotted with the signs of former small scale mining use. Although the bell pits had been filled in long ago the soil had settled to leave the usual indentation in the ground. I stayed well clear of them as the surrounding wooden fences told me that the area could still be unsafe and if I went down one of these shafts it would be game over and no one would ever hear of me again.

So far the only sounds down in this special place had been the rushing water and the man and his dog struggling along the banks. But this somewhat tranquil scene was broken by the loud fluttering of wings high up in the trees. A large bird of some description took to the air, its beating wings startled a Fox which shot out from under a nearby Holly bush. This in turn alerted the Jack Russell who tried to give chase which led to the man being pulled headlong into the brook. It was worth getting a soaking though to catch a glimpse of the Fox as it climbed the valley side before disappeared into the bushes at the top.

I needed to allow the sun to dry me out so I left the valley at this point and made for another set of open pastures. Taking the opportunity to check the map on my Smartphone I noticed I was not far from the famous but sadly dilapidated Scout Hall. The black cows in the field paid us no attention as we walked carefully along the edge heading for another small footpath that would lead us along the valley where we could once again cross the brook before heading upwards towards Scout Hall.

The stone flagged footpath wound its way up the lower slope of the valley towards the strangely semi-derelict and brooding Scout Hall. The whole area was eerily quiet and as I sat on a low dry stone wall to eat my peanut butter sandwiches my imagination started to wander with thoughts of the stories that I had read about the various ghosts and strange happenings at this place. Although there is a modern farmhouse quite close by the area did give off something of a desolate atmosphere and when a sudden breeze came from nowhere and wafted through the nearby bare trees I decided it was time to pack up and move on.

Scout Hall stands on a small hill on the south side of upper Shibden Dale. The history of the site can be traced back to 1315 when the Stancliffe family were the owners. The name Stancliffe, or Stanclift, comes from the Old German/Old English word for a stone cliff. By Elizabethan times, there were two large houses here. There is no date on the present building, but a nearby cottage has the date 1661 inscribed on it, and a sundial plate shows the year ANNO 1617. The building itself is a large three storey, fifty-three room, four square building built and owned by the Mitchell family in the late 1600s. It has a mixture of architectural styles, from Jacobean, Caroline and Georgian to Italianate, gabled at one end and hipped at the other. It is thought by some to be a Calendar building - its twelve bays representing the months, the 52 doors the weeks and the 365 windows the days. In the late 1940s/early 1950s, the building was converted into tenements and the interior was neglected.

Although there has been a building on the site since the early 14th Century, the current structure was erected by notorious local clothier John Mitchell in 1681. John Mitchell was certainly a curious character. A gentleman silk-merchant, he was known to organise horse races on the nearby moors and was fond of hunting. Mitchell died at the young age of thirty-seven. The man had been obsessed with building flying machines, and boasted that he would one day "fly with the steadiness and velocity of an eagle".

Local tradition records that he was killed in just such a flight attempt from a nearby hill. Some local people say that a phantom flying machine is still sometimes said to be observed overhead in the Shibden valley, followed by a resounding clangour, much like some "heavy contraption falling from a great height on rocks". Meanwhile, several previous tenants of the Hall have complained of witnessing strange shapes drifting through the rooms and have been disturbed by uncanny noises in the night. In its current state this notion is very believable. By the mid-1980s, the Grade II listed hall was derelict and in a serious state of decay and ruin. It was partially restored in the 1980s, but now seems to be again in a sad state of disrepair.

As I left this desolate and forbidding place and wandered past the Georgian splendour of Lee House nearby, I wondered if the atmosphere at my next point of call could be any more brooding and menacing. The magnificence of the fine cobbles all along Lee Lane brightened my mood somewhat as did the scenery of the far side of the valley as I took to the footpath along the ridge to the cottage and farmstead of Black Boy.

As I wandered along through the trees of the upper slope of the Shibden Valley, I steadied myself in nervous anticipation of standing before the actual birthplace of one of this country's most notorious mass murderers.

Almost all the history books tell us that John Reginald Halliday Christie was born in Halifax, some say that he entered this life at Northowram, and one or two actually name the place as Black Boy House. Making my way along the sharp cobbles of Hag Lane I did wonder if I was walking in the footsteps of the man himself. A ghoulish notion admittedly but life is about dark as well as light and a little of each helps to broaden the canvas on which to spread my words.

John Reginald Halliday Christie (8 April 1899 – 15 July 1953), known to his family and friends as Reg Christie, was an English serial killer active during the 1940s and early 1950s. He murdered at least eight people – including his wife, Ethel – by strangling them in his flat at 10 Rillington Place, Notting Hill, London. Christie moved out of Rillington Place during March 1953, and soon afterwards the bodies of three of his victims were discovered hidden in an alcove in the kitchen. Two further bodies were discovered in the garden, and his wife's body was found beneath the floorboards of the front room. Christie was arrested and convicted of his wife's murder, for which he was hanged.

Christie was hanged at Pentonville Prison on 15th July 1953. His executioner was none other than Albert Pierrepoint, who actually lived in Clayton on the other side of Queensbury. After being pinioned for execution, Christie complained that his nose itched. Pierrepoint assured him that "It won't bother you for long"

The Christie family came originally from Scotland and came to Halifax via Kidderminster, Worcestershire, where his grandfather was sent as an apprentice in the carpet trade. In 1877 Christie's father, Ernest, brought the family to Halifax, where he became a designer at the renowned carpet making firm John Crossley and Sons at Dean Clough. The family lived in Chester Road, Akroydon and Christie himself was born at Black Boy House. The family, though, moved a great deal, from Salisbury Place, Akroydon, and Queensbury, Iona House, Boothtown, and eventually back to Chester Road.

He was a nervous child who hid under the sheets at night, a habit that continued in later life. And a pivotal moment in his early life came when, at the age of eleven, he was taken to see the body of his grandfather, David Halliday, who had died at the Christie home after a long illness.

The corpse was laid out on a trestle table in the parlour and the sight made a profound impression on the young John. He later recalled: "All my life I never experienced fear or horror at the sight of a corpse. On the contrary I have seen many and they hold an interest and fascination over me."

As I stood there outside the house of his birth I wondered if it was indeed here that Christie had seen his Grandfathers dead body which could have been the tipping point perhaps for him to embark on his sordid career of depravity. But a house is just an assembled collection of stones and bricks and can no way be blamed for the actions of man especially when the crimes are committed many miles away. The building itself just appeared like any other remote but comfortable family home. Washing on the line outside, a Collie guarding the gate and piles of chopped logs stacked neatly by the side.

No rain-laden clouds sending down stabbing shafts of lightning were witnessed, no manic howls of perverted laughter emanated from the cellar. I stared intently for an age at the front room window searching for signs of a grotesque pleading face but there were none. It was simply a quaint old cottage on the upper slopes of the Shibden Valley. What an anti-climax I muttered to no one in particular, and feeling somewhat disappointed, I reeled Lou Parson in and set off down the track towards Halifax.

I thought I had finished for the day but then I remembered a place that I had read about that stood down in the valley a short distance away. I had to walk a couple of hundred yards to find a section of barbed wire fence where I could easily climb through to enter a sloping field. As usual Lou Parson pulled like a train due to the downward slope and within two minutes or so we were once again on the valley floor.

In a small copse on the flanks of the Shibden Valley, no great distance from the Godley Cutting, stands an incongruous building with a Classical facade and some forty yards above it, a three-storey Georgian-style edifice. These structures are the legacy of a spa resort popular in the 18th and 19th Century which exploited a natural mineral spring in the hillside, known as one of the strongest in the country. A variety of medicinal benefits were claimed for it and it's recorded that people travelled from miles around to take the waters.

The spa house itself was built circa 1780 by landowner James Drake (although it is interesting to speculate whether its use for healing had an older provenance as a holy well). Local physicians such as Dr. Robert Alexander would recommend its use to treat a range of complaints including diabetes, poor circulation and digestive complaints. Such was the draw of the resort, Upper Spa House had to be constructed around a decade later to accommodate the growing number of visitors coming from across the north of England.

Dr. Thomas Garnett of Harrogate visited the establishment in 1790 and subsequently published the pamphlet "Experiments and Observations on the Horley Green Spa, near Halifax" in which he observed, "The Horley Green water is quite pellucid – sparkles when poured out of one glass into another – and has a sharp, aluminous, styptic taste, not unlike ink. The taste is not unpleasant when the water is taken from the springhead and drank immediately; but if taken only a few yards from the source its taste is more disagreeable".

The popularity of the spa in the late 18th Century was clearly short-lived and it had apparently fallen into dereliction by 1840. However, the Victorian craze for hydrotherapy led to its restoration by Dr. William Alexander, grandson of its earlier champion Dr. Robert Alexander. The reopened spa also included a bath-house for full immersion in the waters, enclosing the spring in a trough 14 x 12 feet long and 3.5 feet deep.

It is not recorded how many years the site operated under William Alexander's guidance but inevitably, the spa fell into dereliction again once modern medicine had largely discredited the efficiency of hydrotherapy treatments.

But sadly I never reached this place as when I came to the nearby farmhouse the gate was guarded by a severe looking mountain of a man and four very large evil looking dogs. This was enough to convince me to carry on the cobbled track back alongside the valley towards the bustling Godley Cutting and from there to drop down the hill into Halifax where I could catch the bus home.

As I sat in the bus station waiting for the bus it occurred to me that this was the first time I had been down this side of the valley since I completed the fourth walk for my planned historical walking book based on the Calderdale area. This was six months ago and I had shelved work on it due to the ankle injury picked up on Blackstone Edge and the coming onset of winter.

This book on the Queensbury area was intended to fill time until I could once again pick up with my Calderdale book. I smiled to myself when it occurred to me that I had only a few more walks left to complete the Queensbury book then I could be back in the wild, open and inspiring spaces of Calderdale.

Littlemoor and the Spirit of Elgar

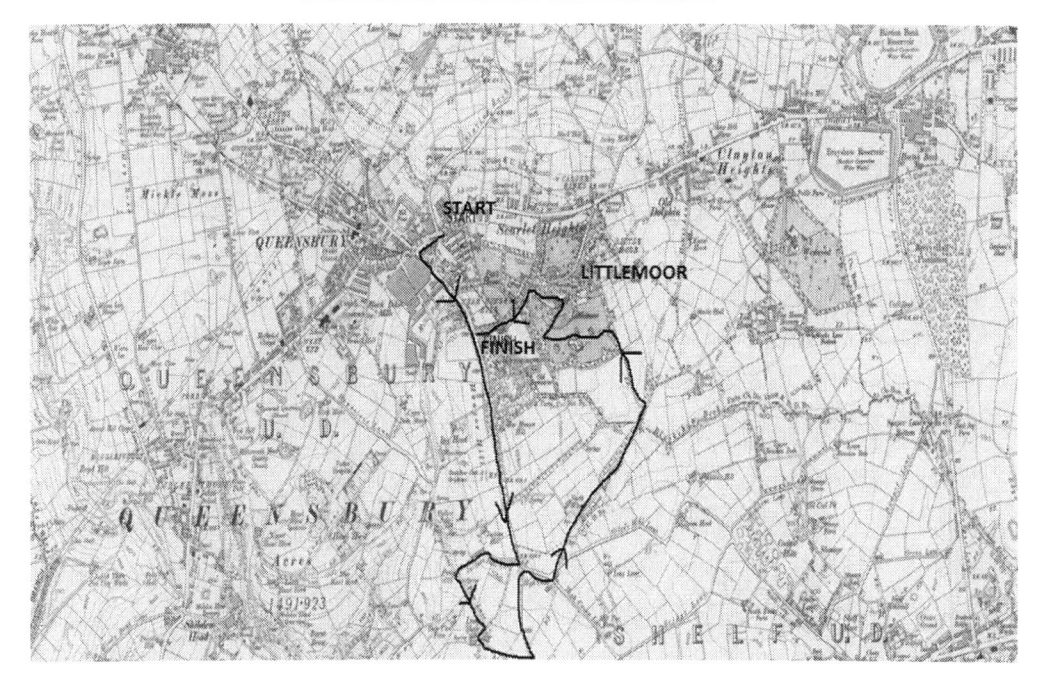

Last night as I lay dreaming

Of pleasant days gone by

My mind being spent on rambling

To the castle I did fly

I stepped on board a vision

And followed the wind of Thor

Till I came to anchor in the trees at Littlemoor

I have had something of a fascination for grand Victorian country houses and their estates ever since I discovered Titus Salt Jnr's lavish pile at Gilstead near Saltaire some years ago. The people that financed and built them are now long gone as are many of the mansions themselves and I think that is a large part of the appeal for me. They represent an age and an ethos that has now been consigned to the annals of our history, but the stories that they convey to us about the people and the times are as relevant today as they have ever been.

The story of Littlemoor Park, the house (hereafter called "Castle") and its owning family the Fosters stands there with the best of them, and this despite there being practically no tangible remains apart from some stone steps and a lodge. That is unless you know just where to look.

There is scant information and a small number of photographs available on the subject of Littlemoor Castle and grounds, and most of this I had avidly consumed as and when I found it. But the layout of the house and grounds became much more apparent when a contact of mine from the Friends of Littlemoor Park was given a hand-drawn map of the area by someone who actually worked there. The map was dated around 1970 and gave certain little bits of information that simply was not available to me up to that time.

Armed with this new information I felt that I was in a position to at last fully explore the grounds where this once magnificent Victorian house stood. This historical walk was the result.

Thursday the twenty-third of February was a dry afternoon even if it was rather cloudy. The ground was still soaked due to the recent heavy rainfall but this did not deter Lou Parson and I from setting out from our base at Sand Beds to start what was to be my tenth visit to Littlemoor. Within a few minutes we were striding along the pavement through Hunger Hill with the fine, long, straight perimeter wall of the Harrowins Estate standing only a short distance away.

Harrowins House was another large house owned by the Foster family and stood for nearly eighty years before being classed as "surplus to requirements" and demolished. Owners included William John Foster (Son of Black Dyke Mills founder John Foster), his Son Robert John Foster and possibly Marc Ernesto Ulysse Marchetti (governing director of Crossley's Carpets in Halifax) Marchetti was the Son of Giulio Marchetti, a talented Italian immigrant who had fought with Garibaldi in the struggle for Italian unification and had later settled in Yorkshire. Giulio married John Crossley's daughter Anne hence the connection to the Halifax carpet empire.

Park Lane also denotes the extremity of the estate along this side and at the corner is the surviving estate lodge. Still looking splendid with its tower, arch and arrow slit windows, the lodge provided a controllable gateway into the Harrowins estate.

The Littlemoor estate can be accessed from the original main gate which still lies halfway along Park Lane but today my intention was to circumnavigate the grounds to the far side where I could enter from such a position where the park would literally lay directly in front of me. The clattering of building work from the new houses within the walls on this side of the estate and the Golf club further on simply did not hold any interest for me although the noise was to play a part a little later on.

After skirting along the edge of the estate for perhaps six hundred yards or so I directed Lou Parson off the main road and down a small footpath that leads along what was once the Southern perimeter. Although we were on a public footpath we still attracted disapproving stares from those with too much money to spend as they idled away their time striking little white balls. The Raggald and the Russell paid them no heed as we were moving on to more important things.

The mansion and grounds of Littlemoor and indeed the Foster family was important to Queensbury and the wider area. The Fosters generated wealth and provided employment for the people of Queensbury and beyond, without them there would have been very little. Their legacy is still evident today through the many fine buildings that still stand in the village, and as much so through those that do not of which Littlemoor Castle was the most substantial.

The assorted noise pollution from the building works still filtered across the still spring air as Lou and I broke out into open countryside. I allowed the leash to reel itself out to its full extent and the lithe Jack Russell needed no second invitation to flex her shoulder muscles and pull me through the damp grass with speed.

I was heading for a spot where I knew the Southern and Eastern corners of the estate came together. A spot where three summers and a thousand years ago I sat eating my dinner on my first ever visit to this wonderful area. That day was at the end of the summer and the main pasture of the estate was being mowed by a tractor with the winter animal fodder piling up behind awaiting collection. I sat on the small stone wall that day for what seemed an age just watching the steel beast working its way around the field, but the impact had already made its mark and I had become somewhat intoxicated by the place.

Reaching the small rickety wooden gate I could now take full advantage of the new and more detailed map donated by the mysterious Mr Fox. Was he once a groundsman, gamekeeper or perhaps a poacher even? Maybe the given name of Fox was a curved ball to throw us off the scent as to who he really was. I didn't really care as he had provided me with information that was invaluable and which had opened up the story of the house and grounds even more. With Smartphone in hand and Fox's map open I took my first tentative steps into the world of Herbert Anderton Foster and crept through the border of mature trees along the Southern edge of the estate grounds.

Herbert Anderton Foster, the grandson of John Foster, was thirty-seven years of age when he commissioned the building of Littlemoor Castle in 1891. He settled late in life, having spent many years travelling the world on his yacht. The Foster family were incredibly wealthy with the success of the mills enabling them to live like kings.

In 1907 he married Frances Edith Agnes Brudenell-Bruce (the daughter of Lord Robert Thomas Brudenell-Bruce) She came with a title and a considerable fortune of her own. Littlemoor, in all its grandeur, was one of a number of properties that the newlyweds owned.

The Victorian mansion itself was designed by the Architects Healey and Healey of Bradford. The architecture was a combination of baronial, and high Victorian gothic and being rich in massive stone work it very much resembled a castle with a fine tower rising well above the rest of the pile, and this will have been the reason for the name given to the building by the local villagers.

The principal rooms were all of noble proportions and the mansion even boasted a long Conservatory or Orangery complete with a Banana tree. The obligatory Billiard room contained a huge organ and even a lift. In one portion of the basement there was a small swimming pool surrounded by white glazed bricks. The house drew gas and electricity from the mill nearby, which enabled it to have all the mod cons that the age had to offer.

The Park itself covered thirty acres and was fully landscaped. Within the grounds stood the Lodges, The Coach House (used as a Fire Station during 1939-1945 war, the Laundry, twenty-two houses, three farms and an engineering workshop. There was also the walled kitchen garden, greenhouses, forcing sheds, flower beds and fruit trees.

I headed towards a small raised mound covered in more mature trees some thirty yards away. According to Fox's map this contained a water feature and was used as a reading area for Mr Foster and his family. Of course the trees are today far more substantial than in years gone by and there is no longer any sort of a bench or seat on which to sit and rest a while. But as I stood amid the trees on the slightly raised mound I could fully appreciate just why this position was chosen for such relaxation.

As I stood there on the mound gazing out across the short spring grass I could barely see what I would only call a "saucer" shape in the pasture before me. Fox's map and the OS map told me this was the position of the famed pond. The same pond that contained small fish such as Sticklebacks and where local children from the village would skate upon in the winter. The shape of the pond is still discernable on the land but if you had no knowledge of the pond's existence then you would see nothing.

Lou and I set off across the wet grass and it was not hard to envisage the village children playing on the ice as they enjoyed the obvious hospitality and generosity of the Fosters. I would imagine they were indeed grateful as were their parents. To the northeast of the ornamental pond stands a clump of nondescript trees. As I walked through here I came to what was due to its shape quite obviously the famed "arched tree tunnel". The thin branches were as yet unadorned with blossom and leaves but their shape created a tunnel through which the Fosters and their sometimes famous visitors could walk to visit the pond.

Walking through this veritable time vortex it was easy to envisage the earthen floor covered in fallen blossoms. The sweet aroma of the petals pervading the nostrils as the summer sun sets on yet another fine day in the lives of the wealthy Herbert Foster and his family. Reaching the far end of the tunnel I spied a conveniently placed rock on which to rest a while. Moments like these are usually the time when my trusty old tobacco tin makes an appearance and this occasion was no exception.

The shafts of smoke drifted around my head but only for an instant as a breeze had suddenly developed from nowhere. The trees around me rustled and the sound covered up the by now faint sounds from the machinery on the new build estate by the main road. Then, as soon as it had arrived the breeze disappeared and madly enough the building noise had dissipated and had been replaced by the faint chatter of what sounded like excited voices. I had not seen anyone on the estate since I had been here and I knew I was alone so it must have been the remnants of the breeze in the trees and bushes surely?

Perhaps the site of the main house had been invaded by other dog walkers whilst I had been down in the main section of the park. Stubbing out my smoke and rousing Lou Parson from her rest I silently made my way up the slight incline and through the bushes towards the large open expanse of grass where the main house once stood. The long, slim and flat lawned area that stood between the house and the stepped terraces is still discernable even today and it was upon this space that in August 1928 there stood a small stage.

Flanked by lines of potted palms, the Black Dyke Mills brass band were tuning up in readiness to entertain the Fosters, their invited guests and assorted local luminaries. Herbert Anderton Foster stood proudly chatting with his most famous guest, the gifted English composer Sir Edward William Elgar. Although I am no student of English classical music I recognised Sir Edward straight away due to his massive but fashionable waxed moustache.

The chit chatter of the surrounding guests faded away and I clearly heard Mr Foster enquire of Sir Edward if he would care to conduct the band during their rendition of perhaps his greatest piece Land of Hope and Glory. Gently grabbing Foster's arm, Sir Edward declared that he would have to decline as he wanted to enjoy their playing instead.

"Perhaps next time I visit your beautiful home Herbie dear fellow, I will lead the band with all the gusto and panache that their skills undoubtedly deserve"

Sir Edward Elgar never got the chance to return as inoperable colorectal cancer was discovered during an operation on 8 October 1933. He told his consulting doctor, Arthur Thomson, that he had no faith in an afterlife: "I believe there is nothing but complete oblivion."

Sir Edward Elgar died on 23rd February 1934. Perhaps the sudden and unexplained breeze amongst the trees and bushes of Littlemoor Park was something more than that. Today was, after all, the 23rd of February.

I had to give my head a shake and make a mental note to not eat so much strong Old Amsterdam cheese so late at night as I wandered off across the expanse of grass that today forms the area where the house itself stood. Here, all signs of the building and its garden fountains and water features are long gone with only a solitary set of stone steps remaining.

Herbert Anderton Foster died aged 76 on the 17th of January 1930 in Perthshire, in one of the other family homes. At that time he no longer needed to live so close to the Mill where he had been a director. In 1936 his widow officially gifted the house to the inhabitants of Queensbury to be turned into a park "to be associated with the silver jubilee of his late majesty King George the Fifth and in memory of the said Herbert Anderton Foster". It is said that the house was constructed with poor quality timber which had decayed over the short number of years of the house's existence, and this was one of the reasons for the gifting to the Council. The Council in their wisdom found it cheaper to demolish it rather than rebuild.

Soon after, in 1937, the house was stripped of all its lavish interior and was extensively altered in the next eighteen months. The grounds became the park we know today and what was left of the castle after the demolition work became a bandstand.

The footprint of the house remained, as did the pretty stone terraces and the steps down to the terraced lawns. It was a nice flat surface on which to play, and was regularly used for racing model cars: the little motors could be heard all across the village. However, beneath the stone floor a network of rooms, including the swimming pool, could still be reached by curious children. They were too tempting, and in 1993, after a young boy was injured playing in the basement, the decision was taken to demolish what was left. Unfortunately the terraces and the base of the round tower went to leaving almost nothing today.

But behind this area deep in the trees are clues if you know where to look and what to look for. The edges of the carriage drive that led to the main door of the house are still visible, the turning circle for the carriages both horse driven then later engine powered can still be seen amongst the trees. The stone bases for the gas lamps that illuminated the driveways at night can also still be seen amongst the layers of fallen leaves. The area where the coaching house and stables once stood is now but a bare patch amongst the trees but with an imagination as vivid as mine it all comes to life.

My mind was swimming with images of dark coaches driven by jet black Geldings as I made my way along the former carriage drive to the main entrance gates on Park lane. The antique gas lamps that I had seen dotted around the gardens of the odd Queensbury residence may well have been the very ones that illuminated the drive along here.

The bright flickering jets of gas brought life to the inky blackness of the wooded parkland and perhaps kept away the odd poacher or shifty looking character.

But not today as the sun was shining and warm as the Raggald reeled in his Russell, stopped and turned around to doff his black flat cap to the memory of the Fosters and the spirit of Sir Edward Elgar before leaving the park and heading for home.

Hanging Falls and the Hill of Squirrels

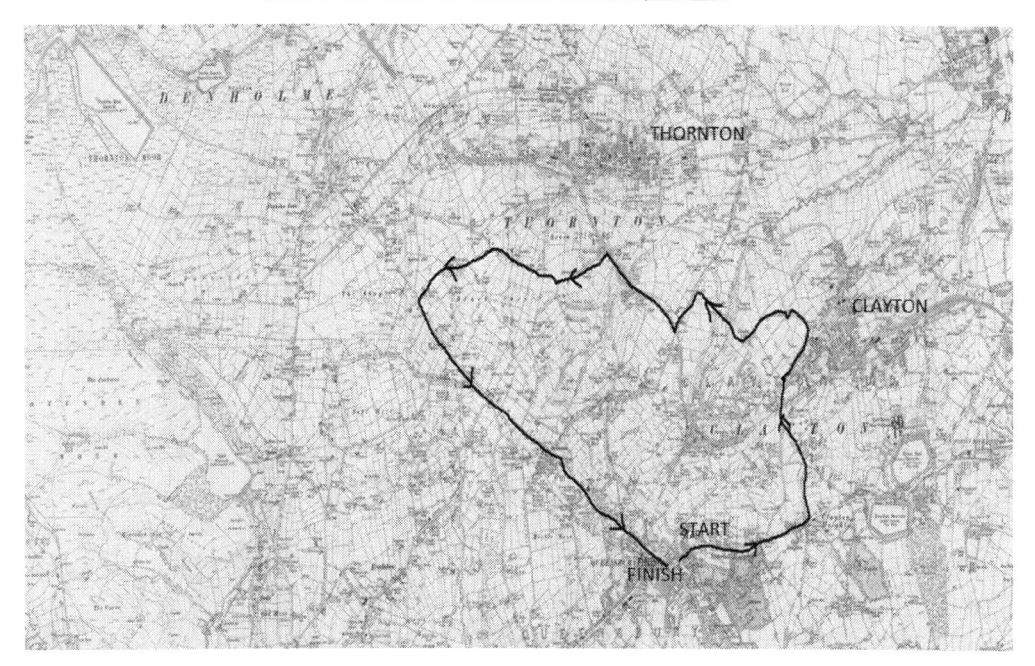

I have always struggled to resist the lure of a mystical and hidden glen. As a badass biker I used to travel many miles to attend rally's and events in this kind of place, but those were days when I had hair and wheels. Today I have neither but I still find my imagination clicking into overdrive when I discover such places. So consider my delight when I discovered not just one but three such places in Upper Bradford-dale. Ok perhaps they are not strictly "hidden" so I use the word just for myself as it conjures up the right sort of image.

The first stop was at the top of the ancient footpath that leads down from the main road at Sand Beds to the Railway Triangle, the very spot where I had fallen in love with the area three years previously. From this sublime vantage point I could gaze out over practically the whole of today's route. It was like having a living and breathing three-dimensional map laid out in front of me. Lou Parson was restless as she always is at this spot for some reason so after a couple of minutes checking my route we set off.

After only a couple of minutes of steady walking we came to the long bony finger of Bright Street. This steep street would not look out of place in San Francisco if it was not for the typical Yorkshire sandstone terrace houses along its length. It protrudes out into Upper Bradford-dale and the view from the last house must be worth dying for.

The much older row of cottages along the roadside at Scarlet Heights with their window tax avoiding blocked up windows are always a delight to see. There is one particular abode in the centre of this long row that presents a quaint arched window above the front door and a stationary dog in the lounge window. For ages I thought it was real and maybe just a little lazy until the owner told me it was actually a pot dog. Time to visit Specsavers perhaps?

The entrance to Littlemoor Park and the Bridal shop across the road is the point at which Scarlet Heights ends and Clayton Heights begins. It was just past here that I headed to search for a gap in the roadside cottages where I could gain access to the evocatively named Sheep Hill Lane. Although this lane begins as something of a track it quickly changes to a mere footpath. Exactly why there is a 30 MPH sign a few feet in is anyone's guess, but I would surmise that at one time it was a vehicular road used as a shortcut to Back Lane.

After skirting along behind modern day semis and bungalows the footpath terminates on Back Lane opposite strangely enough, Sheep Hill. Here the small coppice of trees is unchanged from a century ago, and it was past the trees that Lou and I took another ancient footpath which would take us down towards the edge of Clayton village. As we descended the hill I glanced over to the left and noticed the small white house that once served as the telephone exchange for the area. Opened as a Telephone exchange in 1937 it served the village well into it was converted into a private dwelling sometime in the early 1980's. The footpath ended on Baldwin Lane at the junction with the access track to the Cattery, Kennels and cottage of the sixteenth-century farmstead of Langberries.

I was in search of yet another tiny ancient footpath. This I duly found just after the junction of Baldwin Lane and Brook Lane, and it would take Lou and I back out into more open fields and towards Hanging Falls and Fall top Quarry. The footpath used to lead out past a small quarry and into wide open pastures but today it is hemmed in on one side by modern day houses. After a few hundred yards Lou and I squeezed through a gap in the boundary wall and started across the field. She stopped, turned round and shot me the look that said "let me off the lead Dad, let me stretch my legs, please go on do it do it do it".

"Not a chance, you'll be off at the first sight of anything moving" said I laughing.

Hanging Falls is a rocky outcrop that overlooks Hole Bottom valley. It appears to simply hang there and that I suspect is the origin of the name rather than any connection to the profession of the famous Pierrepoint family from the nearby village.

It was here that I got my initial glimpse of the first of Upper Bradford-dale's famous hidden and mystical glens. And as usual with these things the sun made another striking appearance from behind the large cloud and illuminated the valley below. The pasture in front of me sloped down perhaps some two hundred feet towards the valley floor. Here Hole Bottom Beck gushes its way North East to join Clayton Beck before in time joining other small watercourses to become Bradford Beck. From such a lofty vantage point I could clearly see the iron oxide staining the water a brown orange colour.

This ochre colouring originates deep underground and is often associated with historic mining activity. When washed out of the rock, 'ferrous' iron reacts with oxygen and water and forms 'ferric hydroxide' particles which join to form a thick layer of sediment. This can often smother the riverbed, quickly turning the water into something resembling gone-off carrot soup. The deposits here at Hole Beck are amongst the most striking I have seen and are akin to similar deposits in Heaton Woods which is not a million miles away from here.

The footpath led Lou and I along the edge of Fall Top Quarry where evidence of past industrial endeavours can still be clearly seen. The high-quality stone was in great demand and all the delving was done by hand. It was extremely hard and quite dangerous work. The Foulds family owned this quarry and they employed about thirty people at one time, mainly labourers, including several Irish labourers from Bradford. Much of the stone was used for gravestones in Bowling, Thornton and Scholemoor. The clay was used by Clayton Brick & Stone Company, and a large amount of stone was sold in other towns, and some exported when transport became easier.

It was time to descend down the valley side towards the beck at the bottom. This was easier said than done as Lou Parson was her usual energetic self and proceeded to drag me down at a great pace. The surface was slippy with dew and it was all I could do to remain upright and on my feet. Needless to say we made the bottom in about thirty seconds flat and I only avoided a ducking in the ochre red water of the beck by clinging onto a tree as it whizzed past. As I paused to catch my breath I decided it was time for a rest and a smoke beside the babbling waters in the mystical hidden valley.

From here the landscape around me reared up to create a feeling of enclosure even though the area was vast. So much history and industrial heritage occurred within this "bowl", so much in fact it was hard to take it all in and make much sense of it.

Lou Parson was captivated by something moving in the beck beside us. Not being a lover of water she was initially reluctant to investigate but soon found her courage and stepped in a started thrashing about after a small Stickleback. The fish of course had the edge on her and after taunting the dog for a moment swam away towards Clayton. Naturally I was drenched by the resulting cascade of ochre red water and my one smoke was ruined.

It was time to leave this spot and looking up I could see the steep valley side rearing up before me. It is always harder to climb than to descend and this is where the limitless and abundant energy of the Jack Russell comes into its own. All I had to do was put Lou on a short leash and whisper the word "Pussycats" and she would literally drag me up the valley side towards Cocking Lane. Past the farmstead of Sun Wood we flew and in only a couple of minutes we had reached Cocking Lane Farm.

Oh what joy to be walking nice and easy along the level terrain of the former railway line. Excuse the pun but we flew past the assortment of caged Hens and Chickens that straddle the trail at the site of the former Clayton Fire Clay Works on the embankment at High Birks. Constructed to cross the Birks valley, subsidence was a big problem in constructing this 900ft long, 104ft high embankment, which contained 250,000 cubic yards of tipped material.

We soon came to Headley Lane and here Lou and I turned left beside more babbling water as it sprang from a nearby spring. The road followed a slight incline as it passed what is probably the saddest looking and unloved cottage in the area. Actually a row of three early eighteenth-century cottages it is the end one that is in need of most restoration. What a fantastic and atmospheric home this would surely make if it was brought up to modern day standards.

Across the road stands Headley Hall, which dates from 1589 and is amongst the oldest dwellings in the Queensbury area. Built by the Midgley family in the reign of Elizabeth I, this remarkably unaltered two-storey building constructed in coursed Gritstone with a stone slate roof is today occupied by some very fortunate people indeed.

The gabled west wing has moulded saddle stone and capped shaped kneelers; the left hand one inscribed W Midgley, the right hand dated 1589. The porch is dated 1604 and the stone slate roofs are complete with nineteenth-century corniced chimneys.

The entrance front has a particularly good sequence of chamfered mullioned-transomed windows most unusually retaining their original leaded glazing and wrought iron casements. The main hall window with drip mould, has two rows of eight lights with leaded panes of rare design. I would have loved to have lingered for longer to admire this marvellous historic building but Lou and I were being watched by a face from behind one of the upper mullioned windows in the West wing. Experience and instinct told me our presence here was not appreciated, and not wanting to annoy anyone for a change I sadly set off up the road towards our final destination of the hill of Squirrels.

Continuing along Headley lane between lush green pastures on one side and the greens of the Golf course on the other, we made steady progress. The men playing the one game that I cannot understand paid us no heed as they seemed too busy conjuring up the usual business deals and such like. This suited me as I have very little to say to them apart from just make sure you pay your correct amount of taxes.

The Raggald and the Russell arrived safely at the junction with Malt Kiln Lane and Pit Lane in one piece. From this point I could see the village of Thornton nestled on the hillside behind us, the Speak Institute away on the horizon in front, and isolated farmhouses dotted on the land in between. Along this stretch of road lie two old properties each with the name Malt Kiln. The nearest one being named "Far" if that makes sense and the other simple Malt Kiln.

A Malt kiln was a facility in which barley, etc., is dried after steeping and germinating. The grain was then allowing to sprout and then dry to stop further growth. The malt was used in brewing beer, whisky and in certain foods. The traditional malt house was largely phased out during the twentieth century in favour of more mechanised production.

The grain was first soaked in a steeping pit or cistern for a day or more. This was constructed of brick or stone, and was sometimes lined with lead. It was rectangular and no more than 40 inches deep. Soon after being covered with water, the grain began to swell and increase its bulk by twenty-five percent.

The cistern was then drained and the grain transferred to another vessel called a couch, either a permanent construction, or temporarily formed with wooden boards. Here it was piled 12–16 inches deep, where it began to generate heat and start to germinate. The grain spent a day or two here, according to the season and the Maltster's practice.

The grain was then spread out on the growing floor, the depth dictated by the temperature, but sufficiently deep to encourage vegetation. It was turned at intervals to achieve even growth and over the next fourteen days or so it is turned and moved towards the kiln. The temperature was also controlled by ventilation. A day or two after the grain was turned out on to the floor, an agreeable smell was given off, and roots soon began to appear. A day or so later the future stem began to swell, and the kernel became friable and sweet-tasting. As the germination proceeded the grain was spread thinner on the floor. The process was halted before the stem burst the husk. At this stage much of the starch in the grain had been converted to maltose and the grain was left on the floor to dry. The art of malting depends on the proper regulation of these changes in the grain. Maltsters varied in their manner of working, and adapted to changes in climatic conditions.

The barley was then moved into the kiln for between two and four days, depending on whether a light or dark malt was required. A slow fire was used to start, and then gradually raised to suit the purpose of the malt and the desired colour. The barley was then sieved to remove the shoots and stored for a few months to develop flavour. The finished Malt will have been used in the production of Beer in the many local breweries which were dotted around the Queensbury area in the last century.

Many villages had a Malthouse in the eighteenth century, supplying the needs of local publicans, estates and home brewers. Malt houses are typically long, low buildings, no more than two storeys high, in a vernacular style. The germination of barley is hindered by high temperatures, so many malthouses only operated in the winter. This provided employment for agricultural workers whose labour was not much in demand during the winter months.

As Lou and I reached the farmstead and cottage of Green Head Clough, we turned up along Deep Lane onto Squirrel Hill. The mere mention of the word Squirrels is enough to lead Lou Parson into something of a frenetic giddy dance of sorts. The country lane was quiet and devoid of traffic so I let the leash run out to its full fifteen feet, and this allowed the mental Terrier to not only pull to the front like a train but also swing from side to side as she inspected each hedgerow for the presence of Squirrels. For such a small dog she possesses power and energy way beyond what is normal even for a Jack Russell. So it was with something of a sense of relief when we passed Keelham Farm Shop and reached the main Brighouse and Denholme Road.

As Lou Parson and I started the linear walk back to Queensbury I was on the lookout for a particular roadside cottage. A friend of mine had recently told me a tale that his Father had told him many years ago. The story was that an unnamed man once lived in a cottage along this stretch of road. The only information I had about the cottage was that it had an "unusual" Gable end.

The man in question was a "Gentleman Jewel thief and burglar", a Raffles type character Barry told me. He was so slick and professional the law never proved anything on him and he escaped justice. I had also been enquiring about him to most people I had contact with in the Queensbury area since I moved here and not a single soul knew anything about him. I am still looking to this day and I am not sure if he even existed at all.

From here it was a short and straight route back towards Queensbury across Clews Moor, passing by Black Carr Farm, Travis House Farmhouse and the cottages also named Travis. Farming families in this area recall horse drawn sledges being used in the fields until after WW2 due to the boggy nature of the ground. Travis House Farmhouse was built around 1830, and although no properties existed at the time of the 1773 Enclosure Act, the area "Travis" came to include the house, the barn next door(now known as Travis Cottages) and the adjacent row of Low deckers on the site of today's garage.

Resisting the urge to call into the famous Raggalds Inn for a well-deserved beer, Lou Parson and I continued on towards Mountain and the journey back to base at Sand Beds.

My friend Barry has since confirmed to me that the cottage with the strange gable end has been demolished and has been replaced with a newer building. He was puzzled that no one apart from him knew anything about the gentleman jewel thief and took it upon himself to drive along the Brighouse and Denholme Road to search for the cottage. Despite my attempts to dig up some information on this subject the mystery remains unsolved. Like the tale of the "Armoury" from Littlemoor Castle being dumped and hidden in the pond by employees of the estate, I fear it is nothing more than local folklore.

Brow Top Mill and Clayton Railway Tunnel

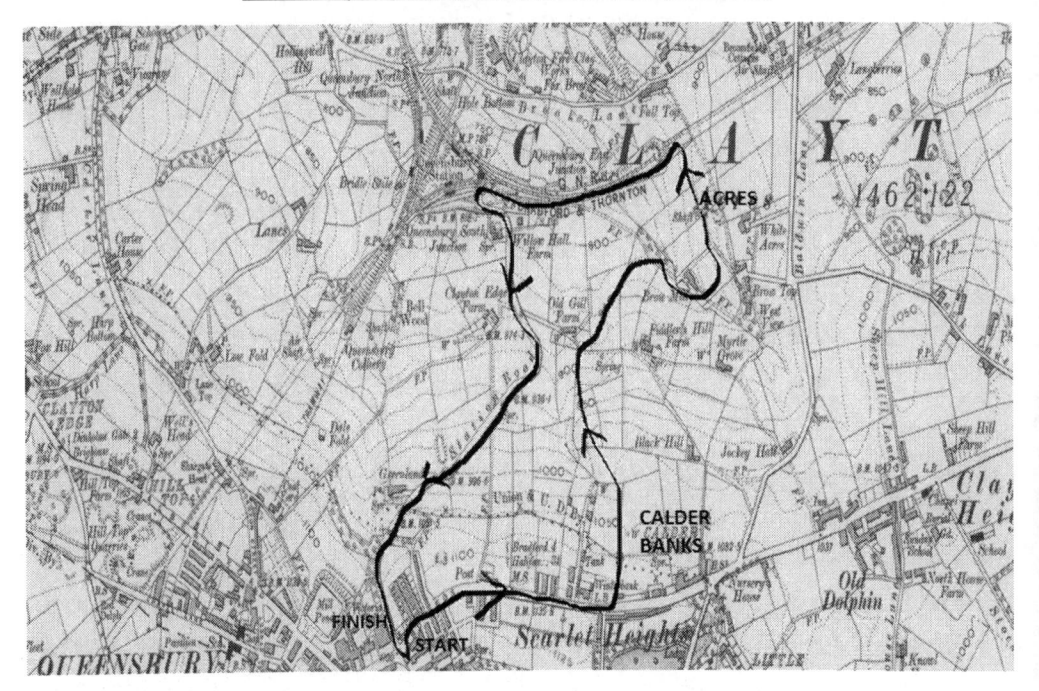

I was asked the other day where I get the inspiration for my historical walks. The old man with the flat cap and scruffy white beard leant forward as he sat on the bench on Roper Lane. Staring straight across the hillside to Bonnet Hall, his lips hardly moved as he spoke to me in a broad Yorkshire accent. I told him that on most occasions it was nothing more than a scrap of information on an old Ordnance Survey map that sparks my interest. I dig a little deeper and stories of people and the past merge together to form what ultimately becomes one of my historical walks.

"Best get on wi it then lad"

"Aye, best I had old man"

This walk to visit the site of an early Victorian Woollen mill in Bradford-dale was indeed one of those occasions. Hidden away in a tiny glen to the north of the dale, the mill site had captured my imagination with the thoughts of dour Victorian working class folk scratching out a meagre living. The presence of the famous Clayton railway tunnel nearby only added to the excitement that mounted as I scoured the Ordnance Survey map to make my plans. Like most people in the area I had visited the entrance of the Queensbury tunnel but never the Clayton tunnel.

The dagger shaped scar on the landscape can clearly be observed from Sand Beds with the tunnel entrance and the in-filled cutting forming the blade with the handle running back to Baldwin Lane.

As usual the ever ready Lou Parson joined me and we set off along the road through Scarlet Heights and beyond to our entry point to the valley below at Calder Banks. Lou didn't need any coaxing to dash down to the field as a passing bus scared her witless and sent her bolting off down the track pulling me with her. I was happy that the grass in the field was not too wet after the recent heavy rain but I knew some areas of the fields below me would be sodden due not to rainfall but due to the many tiny springs that emanate from the hillside.

Passing by the moss and lichen covered stones of a long gone structure of some kind named on the old OS map as Calder Bank, we soon came across the first of these natural springs. Here the grass had been replaced by small reed-like plants and their presence denoted the direction of the water as it burbled down the hillside towards Hole Bottom. I launched Lou over the nearby dry stone wall then clambered over myself to discover the tiny glen where the mill stream flows was still hidden by another hillock. We had to descend another two hundred feet to reach the valley floor where this tiny unnamed watercourse once powered the first mill to be constructed in the Clayton area.

I could now see the small farm at Black Hill away to my right and before long the farmhouse of Old Gill below came into view. Another spring gushed from a crumbling old dry stone wall, the water pooling before sinking into the ground and percolating its way relentlessly downhill to join the mill stream in Hole Bottom. Like veins in an outstretched hand, these numerous springs flow to connect to the becks that line the floor of Bradford-dale. These becks in turn flow into Bradford Beck which ultimately joins the river Aire at Shipley.

Strangely enough Lou Parson showed no interest whatsoever in the skeletal remains of what I was later told to be a Goose in the field. Stripped of its flesh the ribcage laid there in one complete piece with a single leg bone trailing behind. The two wings with their white feathers peacefully in situ laid alongside like they had been placed there in silent tribute.

The small glade of aged trees that straddles the mill stream loomed into view. The stream itself was swollen and fast running due to the recent heavy rain. Producing noise that belied its small stature, the trees funnelled the gushing water towards me. Spotting a crossing point some way down the glade, we headed along the steep muddy bank towards the site of the mill. Even Lou Parson was struggling to keep her feet as we slogged along through the mud. I stopped for a moment to catch my breath and from here I could just make out a vegetation covered stone wall that had held up the field above for perhaps two centuries.

The wall with its sentries of gnarled old trees gave the whole area a feeling of a mystical and forgotten valley. It is places like this that inspire my imagination to run riot, and images of Pixies, Fairies and the odd Elf were not far from my mind as I trekked along the bank. I half expected to see JK Rowling sitting around on a rock somewhere scribbling down ideas for her next book- it was that kind of place.

I have always had something of an interest in the industrial mills of the Bradford area. Not just the well-known examples such as Listers Mill in Manningham or Titus Salt's Mill in Saltaire, but also of the smaller and some would say less significant industrial mills. Brow Top Mill was one such mill but it was important because it was the first mill to be constructed in the Clayton area.

Clayton's textile industry began in the 18th century, with handloom spinning and weaving in the cottages of local villagers. The finished pieces would be sold in Bradford and at the Piece Hall in Halifax. At the beginning of the 19th century Clayton had over a thousand handloom weavers working from home as it were. With the advent of the industrial revolution and mechanisation, the work was transferred into a mill environment and people flocked from the countryside into the slums that developed around the mills in the city centres.

After a short while walking through the mystical glen, I clambered up the banking and managed to make the top after some difficulty. Lou Parson was already in the field above where the mill once stood and I joined her on the access track. The air was still and the only sound to be heard was the gentle burbling of the stream as it went on its way to Hole Bottom to join the beck of the same name.

Brow Top Mill was situated in this small valley below Brow Top Farm. Access for the carts was via the steep lane and farm yard, or by foot via a path leading from Raven Cottage on Brow Lane. The mill itself was constructed of stone and measured seventy-five feet long by twenty-five feet wide. Built over three storeys with a warehouse extending over two cottages it was tiny in comparison with the larger mills that would be constructed in the coming years. Brow Top Mill was built by Timothy Wood in 1823 and in the late 1820's he started in business as a worsted manufacturer. In 1835 the mill was described as having an engine of ten horse power, eleven days work of land, two cottages and a barn.

In 1838 the mill was purchased from Mr Wood by Joseph Fawthrop. The year 1854 was a disastrous year for business, due to the high price of wool and several small firms were ruined. Trade picked up but by 1858 the bad times had returned and Joseph decided to sell. In 1860 the newly formed business of Joseph Benn and Co, leased the mill. The partners, formerly employees of John Foster of Black Dyke Mills were Asa Briggs, Alfred Wallis and Joseph Benn. The company leased the mill for two years before moving to Beck Mill in 1862. The 1861 census shows Joseph Benn living in one of the mill cottages. From 1862 the mill was leased to several companies and was finally sold by the Fawthrops in 1873 to Jaques and Wright & Co. In 1878 it was sold to John Kershaw who in 1882 built West View House at the head of the glade.

In 1907 the mill and West View were again sold in parts to several people. One of which was Sam Priestley of number two Brow Cottages who purchased barns stables and also another cottage number four Brow Top. The mill itself though was now in decline and was used for a time as a rug making works in 1917. The ordnance survey map of 1921 shows the mill as derelict and the Mill was eventually demolished in the early thirties.

As I stood on the spot where the small mill pond once stood and gazed up the field where the access track had been, it was not difficult to imagine the heavy laden carts being dragged up the incline by tired sweaty horses. Young boys were no doubt employed to push from behind to ease the beasts from their burden, but still the lives of the horses from this time would have been abysmal at best.

What was hard to imagine though was the hive of industrial endeavour that occurred on a daily basis on this spot. Small the mill may have been but there will still have been a sizable amount of activity in this area. But today, apart from the babbling of the stream and the hammering of two men on the roof of the distant Fiddlers Hill farm, all was quiet.

After a while and keeping Lou Parson on a short lead, I started to move away from this beguiling little spot. With Lou Parsons's assistance I was able to climb up the steep field and make my way over the valley side towards the huge hump of the Clayton railway tunnel spoil heap. I knew from experience that this kind of industrial monument was usually riddled with Rabbit warrens due to their construction and the nature of the spoil itself. So I reminded myself that my right arm was most likely going to be practically wrenched from its socket as my Jack Russell spied her natural quarry and sets off in chase.

It was like Lou had sensed there was something worth chasing nearby as she led me across three fields to the spoil heap at some speed. Upon reaching it we climbed up the side and from the top I could indeed see that the spoil heap was covered in evidence of rabbit activity. Two small grey creatures darted from a hole a few feet away and like a flash Lou was off. Or so she thought as I had spotted the movement an instant before her and held the lead fast and steady. My ale drinking arm was saved for another day and the Rabbits were safe as I would never allow Lou to actually kill anything. It's the thrill of the chase nothing more.

From my vantage point atop the spoil heap I could see the trajectory of the former track bed as it snaked away towards where the triangular station complex once stood. The only remaining railway building down here is the former Station House. Speaking to the lady who now lives there a short while later on Station Road, it appears to be something of an aged but atmospheric place to live. A place of charm and character and a reminder of a wonderful past.

Upon the demise of the railway, the former railway cutting was in filled to perhaps fifty feet or so from the tunnel entrance. The West portal entrance itself is now bricked up with only a small metal door for access. There was no chance I would be going down there as the sides of the steep drop were covered in bushes and hibernating brambles, and besides the door would be locked.

Clayton Railway Tunnel is a 1,057-yard brick-lined tube which formed part of the rail connection between Bradford and Queensbury. During construction in 1874, Thomas Coates (20) and William Elliot (27) lost their lives when their lifting cage fell down No.1 shaft. Thomas Coates was thrown out of the tub and fell 110ft to his death at the bottom of the shaft. William Elliott died the following day in the Bradford Royal Infirmary. William Francis Taylor and Edward Kates were the engineers on duty, and were changing shifts at the time, which may have had a bearing on the accident. Both casualties are buried in the graveyard of Clayton Parish Church where a headstone commemorates the accident.

Since the closure of the line, the eastern approach to the cutting has been completely filled-in and a housing estate built on the surrounding land. A bungalow sits directly above the portal - its conservatory recently suffered subsidence, possibly due to the void beneath it. Inspections of the tunnel take place annually with access gained through the metal door in the West Portal. It was through here that a Network Rail worker discovered a covert Cannabis growing operation whilst carrying out a routine inspection in June 2012. Police confirmed they got a call reporting the Cannabis factory from a worker who said he had walked about half a mile into the tunnel when he found a tent and inside it five hundred plants and associated equipment.

Both the Queensbury and Clayton railway tunnels were immense achievements even for the seasoned and experienced Victorian Engineers. As I stood looking down at what is left of the cutting onto the West Portal, I wondered if they knew the size of the task they were undertaking when they surveyed the land before them from the Turnpike road up at Sand Beds.

The stone walls that enclosed the cutting are today no more than normal height but before the in filling they stood atop a banking perhaps twenty feet tall. Now they are no taller than a man's height but still they show the trajectory of the long gone line. So dragging Lou away from another rabbit warren I made my way between the aged walls towards the wrought iron footbridge that crossed the tracks at Queensbury East junction. This now sadly rotting structure is the only piece of railway infrastructure that remains in the triangle today.

Stopping to gaze somewhat aimlessly up towards the horizon, I could make out The Speak Institute at Mountain as it stood watching us in silence at the top of the hill with Scarlet Heights Farm up at Sand Beds observing us from the other side. During the course of the afternoon I had dropped down some three hundred feet and in a few short minutes I would have to start the long arduous climb up Station Road towards home.

Lou Parson and I reached the tiny footpath that runs alongside the former Station House and the iron bridge. The last time I walked along here some three years before my footsteps had awoken what had seemed like a whole kennel of noisy dogs at the rear of the Station House. It was like Groundhog Day as once again the building alongside the footpath was shook to its very foundations by the baying of very large hounds. It was not a time to hang about so I hurried Lou along and made it to Station Road in one piece.

I had walked maybe a hundred yards or so up the hideously steep rocky road when a heard a commotion behind me. A woman with two very large dogs emerged from the front of the Station House and headed our way.

She appeared older than me but a little fitter as she strode up Station Road like it wasn't there. Struggling to control the massive Akita and Rottweiler she had in tow she nonetheless closed the gap between us in no time. I moved over to the side of the road to give her more room but already Lou was straining on the leash. They may have been big dogs but Lou Parson was not scared in the least and was merely letting them know in her spitting and snarling way to keep well clear. This they duly did and paid her no attention as the woman greeted us as she reached us. Strange dog this of mine as she does things like that then cowers against the wall when a bus goes past. Jack Russell's sometimes have no rhyme or reason and that's just one aspect of them that I find most compelling. The woman and I had a short conversation about the merits of living in the Station House before she went on her way.

As she continued up the road I tried to match her for speed but it was no good and I had to stop for a breather by the stone bridge abutments that line the road half way up. The two stone abutments were part of an ill-fated never built scheme to link Queensbury Station with the village by tramway. At various times a tramway, and a circuitous branch line, climbing to the town were mooted, but never built. The trudge up the hillside to the village of Queensbury will have seemed as daunting to the Victorians as it does to people today. Well, to me anyway, as it never gets any easier no matter how many times I climb up it.

After a minute or so of filling my lungs with the rapidly cooling air I gathered Lou onto a short lead and set off uphill towards Sand Beds and home. The woman with the large dogs was still in sight in the distance and I matched her stride for stride and we ate up the distance reaching Victoria Hall and the main road in only a few minutes. It had not been the longest walk I had ever done by all means but it had been one that had interested and inspired me greatly. I had discovered and enjoyed one of the three so-called "Hidden Glens" of upper Bradford-dale. Mystical, alluring and historic- it doesn't get much better than that for me.

The Old Man on the Mountain

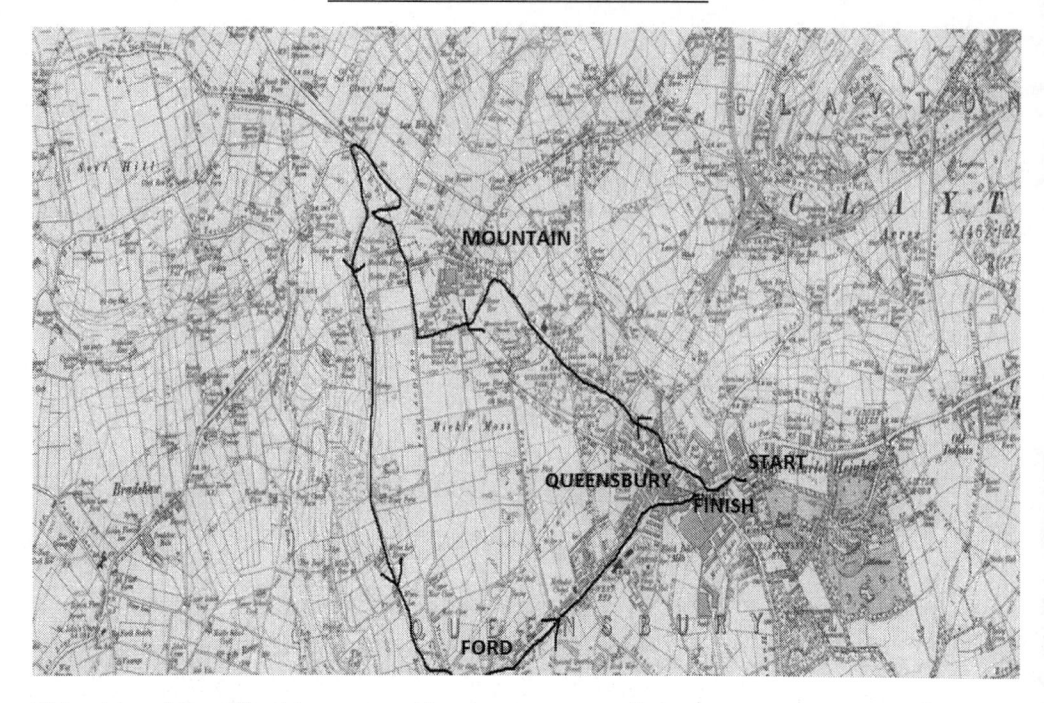

This side of Bradford is covered in strange sounding place names, Bay of Biscay, Egypt and Moscow to name but three. But the one that has always captured my imagination more than most is the name Mountain. It conjures up images of high barren terrain, empty land strewn with rocks and boulders, and snow. Although I have yet to live in this area through the height of a typical Queensbury winter I have no doubt that the hamlet of Mountain fully deserves its name.

It is just as well then that this walk was undertaken on one of the few days in late February where the sun was strong and the wind as light as a feather landing on a maiden's pillow. The evening before was spent noodling over the old Ordinance Servey maps looking at nothing in particular, searching for inspiration and ideas with which to create yet another historical walk. Sometimes that is the way that these things work for me and this time was no different.

I was on the verge of extinguishing the light, bolting the heavy front door and mounting the stairs to make for bed (makes me sound like Scrooge) when my tired eyes chanced upon the words "California Row" on the map. This is Queensbury in West Yorkshire not Los Angeles I said out loud to Lou Parson.

But my interest had been aroused and upon discovering that this place had been consigned to the misty annals of history, I decided to visit the actual spot as it is today and use it as an excuse for another historical walk. So after waiting for Lou Parson's main foe, the Postman, to visit we set off along Albert Road on the trail to Mountain.

After only a short distance Lou and I came to the tiny area known as "Small Page". This was where David Knowles, a rival industrialist of John Foster constructed many properties at a time when his own textile business prospered. His own later residence, Queensbury House stands behind the George III Inn, which was probably his warehouse. All of Knowles's developments in Queensbury can be seen on the map of 1852, before Foster started to build housing on his own land.

An important building in the social development of Queensbury is the Hall of Freedom, built in 1854 by the Queenshead Public Institute in Nelson Street on David Knowles's land. The hall provided rooms for meetings and lectures which were independent of religion and the Foster family and were therefore well used by Chartists who sought to pressurise Parliament into improving the living standards and rights of the workers. A meeting at the hall in 1855 led to the foundation of the Queenshead Co-operative Society.

A little further along Albert Road stands Goodwin House. This modern building stands on the site of what was known as the Navvy Houses. These simple cottages were constructed around 1873-75 to house the Navvies who had come from all over the country to construct Queensbury railway tunnel. They were intended to last for "as long as the job took" but were in fact not demolished until 1961 so actually outlasted the tunnel and the railway.

There were three rows of these back to back houses, numbering 44 in total. They were named Railway Street, Northern Street, Great Street and Oakley Street. For some reason later inhabitants of the Navvy houses tended to consider themselves to be Mountain folk rather than of Queensbury, possibly because several Mountain families moved there after the Navvys left.

As is usual the pavement from Small Page onwards was dotted with seemingly strategically placed piles of Canine crap. Apart from the footpath alongside the edge of Littlemoor Park this stretch of the road appears to be the toilet for most of the village dogs. I must have looked like a Tap Dancer after twenty cups of Coffee as I manically tried my best to avoid the splattered pavement.

Just a short distance past Foxhill School there is a strange little aperture in the stone roadside wall indicates the site of Mountain End coal pit. This was the access for the Colliers and was known as "t'bob'oil" because one had to bend or "bob" under it to get into the pit area. Closing in 1891 the pit site extended from Blind Lane to some way past the school.

By now the pavement had cleared somewhat and Lou Parson and I could make some headway onwards towards Mountain. The view over my shoulder of Bradford-dale was inspiring and invigorating as the sun had broken through the clouds and the whole valley was lit up with its warming life-giving rays.

Only a few hundred yards further along we came to The Speak Institute. Built by local mill owner John Speak in 1913 for £3000 in memory of his father and mother. It was said that the construction was inspired by the building of Victoria Hall in Queensbury and the Institute's purpose was to provide recreational and social facilities for the good folk of Mountain.It has been used for many purposes including a hotel and conference centre and is now a private house. The building was bought in 1989 by Haworth author Stan Ledgard who completely refurbished it and renamed it Mountain Hall before running residential psychic awareness courses there.

The building is complete with a tower that holds a water tank and a cupola. Designed by Herbert Hodgson of Bradford, it stands proud and compact overlooking the main road and within sight and easy reach of Speak's mill.

The Speak family were to Mountain what the Fosters were to Queensbury. They were mill owners and philanthropists but the family was not the creators of Mountain Mills. Construction was begun in 1818 by Isaac Hirst on land he had bought at Mountain, and it was in production by 1821. Terraces of cottages were built nearby to house the workers and in 1844 the mill was purchased by John Clough and his nephew Paul Speak. There were problems at first due to lack of staff as many people had left the area because of low employment. However, in May 1854 Speak bought the mill from Clough and began a period of upgrading and expansion. By 1873 the mill gates and time office and most of the improvements were complete.

The mill was sold to The Parkland Group in 1937 and in the coming years various plots of houses and cottages around the mill were sold off. After cloth production ceased, the mill was divided into units and included a bakery and a double glazing company. In the late 1980's the last of the mill was demolished with some of the stone being used to rebuild the roadside wall along the main road. The mill site was left void for some years until planning was granted for housing.

Lou Parson and I crossed over the main road from the institute and started along Mill Lane. A smart row of Yorkshire stone houses formally named Fascination Place stands on the left right next to a paved track that once led to the mill weaving sheds. At the far end of this row stands the old mill time office and lodge with its foot gate still attached at its side. Two hundred yards further along is a similar row named Luddendon Place and this led us to Old Guy Road. On the corner is a small dirt track that today leads to a large cattle shed. This was the site of the romantically named California Row that I had noticed on the OS map the previous evening. The farmyard on the corner contained two massive snarling dogs of which only one was restrained. Thankfully the other beast was so old it did not have the energy to clear the perimeter wall and simply stood there barking its head off at us. The chained dog appeared to be younger and would have no doubt cleared the wall if it could have done.

Steadying myself once again after the onslaught, I led Lou Parson down the dirt track towards the cattle shed. Here amongst the assortment of modern day farm buildings stood California Row. Shown as a hotch-potch of houses California Row stood on the most exposed part of Mountain. The land was owned by Mrs Lancashire and Mrs Brook who sold off the plots in 1853. The access road was marked out, then the houses built in blocks by the plot owners-first numbers 4-10, then 24-30, then filled in with numbers 16-22.

Numbers 12 and 14 were occupied in 1853 which indicates a quick building job. Number 2 was a "low decker" with the other houses being two-storey through by lights except numbers 26, 28 and 30 which were also low deckers. All the houses had a small garden to the south. From 1976 to 1978 all the houses were purchased by the council and demolished.

The "Cali" is remembered as being "nice houses" during the first half of the 20th century, and housed many members of families with long associations with Mountain-Rushworth, Sutcliffe and Drake. The whole block 18-30 was owned by the Rushworth family from 1875, selling off units as the members died. The last Rushworth was Ida at number 22 from 1937 to 1972. She was a well-respected teacher at the nearby Foxhill school.

The last occupant of number 2 in the 1930's was Miriam Ambler, who was regarded as an eccentric or a witch. At this time, Susannah and Lavinia Barrett took over the tenancy of number 6 on the death of their Father Solomon. The ladies baked and sold excellent pastries at their house, and also supplied Kirkbright's fish shop with pies. The field in front of the Cali. Known as The Moor, was owned (in the 1853/85 period) by Mr Scott of nearby Micklemoss Farm. Originally Cali residents paid him 1 shilling a year to him for the right to hang out their washing on his land.

On the edge of the field at the Raggalds side was a well that was dug by John Willie Sutcliffe. In the field stands a pile rather like the spoil heap from a pit. It is, in fact, mostly horse dung piled over the remains of a stone crusher which was used in the mid-1900's to make sand from waste stone. The area had been a stone quarry in the early/mid-1800's. So despite the name the lives of the residents of California Row will surely have been totally different from what their American counterparts would have enjoyed. Gritty Yorkshire grime and hardship as opposed to warm sun and Palm trees.

The approaching sound of a Land Rover down the dirt track compelled the Raggald to gather up the Russell and decide it was time to leave and move on down the muddy footpath towards Roper Lane. The barbed wire fence at the foot of the sloping field took some surmounting as I caught my arm on the sharp barbs and struggled to free myself for a good few minutes. Safely on the other side Lou Parson didn't dare laugh as Catweazle flailed around like a loony.

It was worth it though as the vista of Soil Hill, Ogden and Bradshaw laid out before me was intoxicating. It was still officially winter but the fields and pastures were bedecked in the lush green colours and shades normally reserved for springtime. Roper Lane shot along the side of the hill straight and narrow like an arrow. Running slightly uphill with Shugden Farm and the site of the long gone Shugden coal pit on its right, Roper Lane would take me on to the ancient settlement of Beggarington, Ford then back to Queensbury.

I had to keep Lou and a short lead and tread carefully along this stretch of road as it was narrow and quite busy with passing traffic. For some strange reason Lou Parson does not like motorbikes and the blat blat sound of an approaching Harley Davidson twin made her scrabble up the steep verge as we neared the crest of the first hill. I heard it coming from miles away and simply revelled in the wonderful noise its two cylinders made as it ate up the tarmac between us.

I carried on up the incline towards Roper Farm. As I rounded the slight bend in the road I could see this distant figure sitting motionless on a small roadside bench. Leaning slightly forward, resting his hands on his knees, he never moved a muscle in the three minutes it took me to reach him. I really thought he was asleep or even dead. I could think of worst places to expire and leave this mortal coil I said out loud to Lou Parson. Still, the old man with the long white hair and the even longer white beard never moved. He just sat gazing out over the valley as motionless as a church Gargoyle.

I didn't know whether to keep on walking right past him or shake him or what. But the decision was made for me as he slowly turned his head towards me as I drew level. I immediately noticed his eyes-they were wide open and bright. Not the usual cloudy windows to the soul that old people normally have when their cataracts develop but wide and clear.

He spoke to the Jack Russell before he acknowledged me. I felt like I was an afterthought and perhaps even should not have even been there. Lou Parson looked up at him and placed her paws on his leg. The old man didn't flinch, he merely moved one hand from his knee and patted her gently on her head.

"I've had a few of these little bastards in my time lad, you've got your hands full I'll tell you that for nowt" he said with a laugh.

"Yeah tell me about it, I wouldn't be without her though old man"

"Funny how they fear nowt but perhaps the odd motorcycle aint it lad?"

How did he know that? We were down the bottom of the hill and round the bend when the Harley passed us and I had not seen him. There were no other roads or tracks around here. Did he have mystical powers or possess the gift of second sight perhaps?

We engaged in a little small talk, mainly about my walking and writing until a thought suddenly occurred to me. If he was that wise and all-knowing perhaps he may know something about the gentleman jewel thief that I had been asking everyone about. So once again I asked the question.

The old man stared straight ahead and was obviously thinking and choosing his words carefully. After what seemed like an age he spoke with a wiseness and authority I had seldom heard before.

"You're not from round here lad that I know because I would know if you were, but have you considered that folk around here might be protecting him eh?"

I too stared across the valley and realised that the old man was not asking me a question but making a statement. I had never thought of it that way and now this strange old man with the bright blue eyes had spoken and it made sense. A response from me was not necessary as I fully understood and I have never asked anyone about Mr Raffles the jewel thief since.

The old man raised his head slowly and exclaimed "rains gonna be coming soon lad, best be on your way now"

For the second time in a few moments I took his advice and stirring Lou from her resting position, headed off towards Beggarington. Still pondering on his words I walked on for perhaps thirty yards then turned and looked back towards the bench where the old man had been sitting. The bench was empty and he had gone. Turning back round again I shrugged my shoulders and continued on. The only sound I could hear in the still cool air was the unmistakable sound of a twin cylinder motorcycle as it receded away into the distance.

Standing on the Top of the World

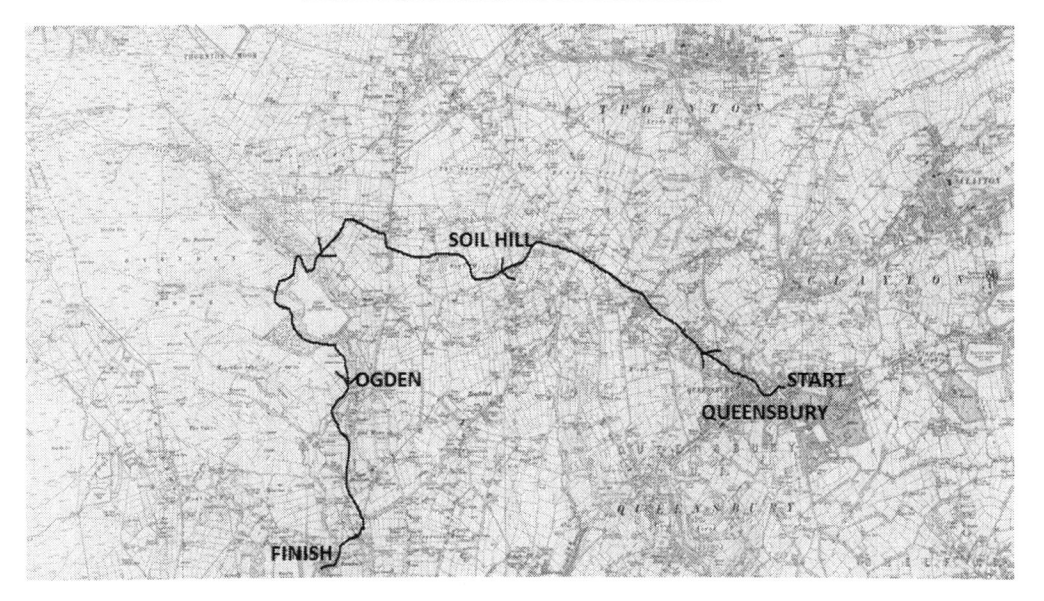

So ok a part of this historical walk consisted of a stroll up Soil Hill and not a fully equipped trek up to the summit of Mount Everest and base camp was at Brickfields not Namche Bazaar but I can dream can't I? At 1300 feet above sea level Soil Hill or Swilling Hill (to use its ancient name) is the highest point in the Queensbury area and naturally as such affords men with nothing better to do views that can only be dreamt about.

Saturday 25th March brought with it some of the warmest and most inviting weather since I had been living in these parts. An early start was in order for Lou Parson and I and we were on the road even before the postman had been. For a change the pavements through Small Page and Mountain were free of dog mess and it didn't take us long to arrive at Perseverance Road or "Mucky Loin"

The object on this road that everyone notices is a boundary stone that stands on the right side after two hundred yards. It commemorates the opening of the road in November 1871 as prior to that date the road was unmade and fully deserved its nickname of "Mucky loin"(lane). This road had long been problematic in winter as run off from the moorland above caused rutting down past the row of cottages. At the bottom, the fields were often flooded, and hence the road too.

The residents of the adjacent houses and farms clubbed together to finance the construction (£75) and this took so long that it was named "Perseverance" Road when it was finally completed. They provided the labour themselves. Today the road appears quite civilised but its long straight rise did give me an indication of how tiresome it would have been to transverse in the days before the modern construction.

After passing the farmhouse of Small tail and its adjacent roadside cottages the road turns left and skirts along the side of Soil Hill. On this stretch of road are the properties of Sun Farm, Millers Row and Cloth Row or Hall as it is known today. Sun Farm was formally known as "Charnocks" after the family who occupied it in the 1700's. From the early 1800's t 1906 there was a Beer House at the farm, originally called The Gin pit and latterly The (Rising) Sun. Its time of glory was perhaps in 1803 when it was chosen as a beacon site in case of invasion by Napoleon.

I was on the lookout for a track that leads off the road up towards the summit of Soil Hill. I knew from a previous walk in this area that this track would take me to one of the few complete Dew Ponds in not just this area but the wider area as well. As I urged Lou Parson through the metal barrier across the track I resisted the temptation to spin around and take in the view down across to Windy Bank. I wanted to wait till I reached the top of the hill and savour the vista in all its glory.

For some reason Lou Parson upped her game at this point and started to pull me up along the track towards the summit. She must have sensed something to chase and perhaps some animal trails that I was of course totally unaware of. As we neared a small pool in the centre of the track she stopped and stared intently at something along the pools edge. I had not seen Frogspawn since my childhood days and it was something that Lou Parson had certainly never seen before. But here was this intuitive little dog staring into a patch of this stuff like she was a Scientist from Cambridge University. It was a good job we were alone as the spectacle of a middle-aged bald man and his dog staring at the earth at nothing in particular may just have looked a bit strange to anyone who was there to witness it.

The Dew Pond stood only a few feet away and, surrounded by its defence of small standing stones it stood out in this somewhat barren landscape. The flat stones are arranged in such a way as to preclude larger beasts such as cattle from entering the pond and destroying its bottom layer therefore allowing the captured moisture to dissipate. Smaller animals like Sheep can access the water through the narrow entrance point.

A dew pond is an artificial pond usually sited on the top of a hill, intended for watering livestock. Dew ponds are used in areas where a natural supply of surface water may not be readily available. They are usually shallow, saucer-shaped and lined with puddled clay, chalk or marl on an insulating straw layer over a bottom layer of chalk or lime. To deter earthworms from their natural tendency of burrowing upwards, which in a short while would make the clay lining porous, a layer of soot would be incorporated or lime mixed with the clay.

The clay is usually covered with straw to prevent cracking by the sun and a final layer of chalk rubble or broken stone to protect the lining from the hoofs of sheep or cattle. To my knowledge it is the only Dew Pond that remains in a complete condition with surrounding stones anywhere around these parts.

This are of Soil Hill is popular with bird watchers or "Twitchers" as that are known, but today Lou and I were completely alone in this lofty landscape. The air was still and silent and this only served to enhance the feeling of isolation that I felt as I climbed up the small hillock that stands close by to the Dew Pond. From here I could clearly make out the far away shape of Idle Hill in the distance. The massive chimney of Listers Mill in Manningham was also visible as was Salts Mill in Saltaire. The view was simply stunning from here as the fields and countryside just seemed to open up down in front of me.

It is said that on a clear day no less than three of England's National Parks can be seen from here. The Peak District to the south, The Yorkshire Dales to the north and in the very far distance The Hambleton Hills on the edge of the north Yorkshire moors. I could also clearly see the pottery works just down the far side towards the main road of Long Causeway.

Between the sixteenth and nineteenth centuries, Soil hill was one of the busiest coal mining areas in the Halifax coal bed. The circular remains of the tops of the old pit shafts are still visible on its slopes. The coal was near to the surface and provided a ready supply to the local industries.

Another of Soil Hill's greatest virtues was the certain type of clay that laid underneath the soil and top turf along its summit. This substance was ideal for making pottery amongst other things and the last remaining Potter working from the Kilnworks down on the Ogden side was a man named Isaac Button.

Built around 1900, this brick building with Welsh slate roof runs east-west adjacent to east end at the top of the hill slope. Within the western part was a bottle kiln with internal radial walls and six segment- arched fire holes around the perimeter. Four flues from beneath the kiln floor run up the hill to the square chimney. Two of these heated the drying shed adjacent to the kiln and two heated a parallel pent-roofed shed where clay slurry was dried before forming. This method of firing and ventilation and the use of waste heat to dry slurry represent an important innovation in earthenware manufacture.

Button was one of the last true English Country Potters and he was renowned for making a ton of clay pots in any 1 day. In fact, he was once timed from throwing the lump of clay onto the potter's wheel, producing an excellent pot and then cutting it off using a wire cutter which in total took him 22 seconds. This would translate into 120 pots in any one hour and up to 1200 in any one day.

By 1900 England had only around 100 country potteries and sadly by the end of the depression no more than a dozen. At Soil Hill there had been a pottery facility since the 17th century and before the First World War this pottery shop employed thirteen men. As time passed, Mr Button ended up working the pottery business on his own because he could not find anyone to take an apprenticeship with him. He passed eighteen years there on his own.

Back in the past this side of Soil Hill will have been a veritable hive of activity with old Isaac amongst others throwing his shapes onto the rapidly spinning potter's wheel. Looking down the hillside at the now dilapidated pottery works it was easy to imagine Isaac weighing out the clay using a large set of scales. He shapes it into one small ball and one large ball. He lifts a large vat from one side of the workshop to the other. Making a base out of the small ball of clay on the wheel, he places the larger ball on top and begins to mould it into a vat, smoothing the edges with the card and making a funnel at the top. He then cuts the vat from the wheel with wire and uses a crescent bracket to help him lift it to the work bench. Large pots with handles are lined up on the shelves in the kiln. Isaac breaks pieces of clay into smaller sausage shapes, and with the slip, places the pieces of clay onto either side of a finished pot. He shapes them over the top to create a handle.

I had spent long enough dreaming on the top of the world and it was time to slowly descend down past the pottery and leave the ghost of Isaac Button behind. Passing banks of Heather, Lou and I were soon at the roadside and making our way over the fields towards the majestic body of water known as Ogden Reservoir. A track led us to New Moss Farm then we joined the short remains of a Roman road as it shot like the proverbial arrow across the fields towards the heavy woodland that surrounds the reservoir.

The moss covered ruins of a long gone cottage named Spring Head can still be clearly be seen amongst the mature trees that populate this section of the woodland. Up to this point on this walk I had not encountered any fellow human beings since I left base camp at Brickfields.

This all changed here in the woods as the loud excited screams and laughs of families enjoying the wonderful natural surroundings broke the silence. Dogs barked excitedly as they ran and scented the many trails that undoubtedly pervaded this entire area.

I knew from experience that most of these dogs that I could hear would be unleashed. I also knew that Lou Parson would bare her snarling teeth at them if they stuck their faces too close to her. How right I was!

As we journeyed around the paths that circumnavigated the reservoir just about every breed of dog you can imagine came up to Lou and every single one was sent packing. Having said that none of the dogs were aggressive in any way, they were only saying hello in their canine way but Lou appears to not tolerate most other dogs invading our space these days. She is simply protecting me as I protect her nothing more than that.

OgdenWater is a 34.5-acre Reservoir surrounded by 174 acres of mixed mature woodland and open moor. The construction of the reservoir was started in 1854 by Halifax Corporation to augment the general water supply to the town. The scheme employed five hundred men and took until 1858 to complete. Holding nearly 222,000,000 gallons of water and standing over 300 metres above sea level the reservoir is capable of supplying the needs of the town by gravity alone.

The woodlands that surround the reservoir were planted in 1905 with some planting and felling around WW2. The dominant tree in the woodland is Scots Pine, with Larch, Sycamore, Beech and Silver Birch also commonplace. Many people have visited this place over the years and a fair few have had benches placed around the water's edge with their names on them in remembrance after they had died. I have found this to be commonplace around the many scenic reservoirs in the West Yorkshire area that I have visited on my travels.

As I approached the concrete embankment at the far side I caught a faint whiff of freshly brewed coffee in the air. That, along with the aroma of freshly baked bread and cut grass are surely amongst the most heavenly of smells a man's nose can detect. The smell could only be coming from a small café and shop on the far side and it was here that I headed to quench my thirst and take a rest for a while.

The two little old women who run the café on a volunteer basis were chatty and friendly and even Lou seemed to be at ease with them. I allowed them to feed her a few bits of their cake they were so lovingly carving up for the days visitors. Lou devoured the pieces like she had not eaten since we left home. She hadn't as I hadn't and this was a perfect time to stop and have my usual famed cheese and onion sandwiches. The coffee was good as well and before long the Raggald and the Russell bid farewell to Dick and Liddy and crossed back along the embankment again.

From here a small footpath skirts along the side of Black Hill. The mud created by the recent rain was already starting to solidify due to the warm sun and the passage was easy. A few isolated cottages lay sprinkled across the far side of the ravine and a busy mill stream wound its way along the bottom. Evidence of the former textile industry can be found along many stream and becks in Calderdale. This particular stream fed the workings of one such mill named Bottoms Mill, a Worsted spinning mill dating from the early 1800's. Though now overgrown, it provides a good example of the feature necessary to power a mill by water. The embankment across the stream created a dam giving control over the water flow. The position of the wooden Goit, which fed the water wheel, and the position of the former wheel are still visible down in the bottom of the ravine.

Lou Parson and I eventually surfaced on the pristine carpet like putting green of Halifax Golf Club. This course was created in 1901, originally with nine holes, and responded to a rise in popularity of Golf around this time. The clubhouse was built on the site of some old cottages in 1902 and the course soon after extended to a full nineteen holes.

Cue more disapproving stares from the assembled Golfers as the Raggald sarcastically doffs his cap and bows before leading his tenacious Terrier off the premises. Although I don't like the game I do like to hack them off by interrupting things somewhat. The remains of a dumped Cannabis grow operation just in the bushes by the entrance to the course made me smile even more.

Union Lane led to Rocks Lane and before long, Lou and I had passed the hamlet of Lower Brockholes and were heading for Mixenden. I resisted the temptation to have a wander around to look for the famed "Mixenden Hoard" as time was marching on and I had a bus for Halifax to catch.

In the 15th / 16th century, there were tales of a buried hoard at Hunter Hill, Mixenden. An expedition in 1510 failed to find anything. The treasure-hunters – who hailed from Bingley – were said to have used black magic to find the hoard. When the church heard this, the men were forced to do penance at local fairs.

Walking along Mill Lane I suddenly remembered the tale of the Mixenden riot. It happened on Hays Lane which upon consulting the map on my Smartphone, I discovered was only around the corner. In 1896, a young man called Varley was charged with raping Sarah Ann – daughter of engine tenter Peter Webster of Hey's Lane, Mixenden. He was sentenced to seven years' imprisonment.

On the evening of Wednesday, 5th August 1896, a group of locals who knew the man and the girl – and her reputation – protested at the sentence, and stormed the girl's home, throwing tin cans and stones at the house. Webster and his four sons were afraid to leave the house to fetch the police. The girl and her mother hid in the cellar as windows were smashed and the house damaged.

Several people were charged with riotously and tumultuously assembling and doing damage to the house of Sophia and Peter Webster:

Fred Rushworth [aged 20] (butcher) - sentenced to 3 months' imprisonment

Herbert Ambler [aged 24] (clogger) - sentenced to 4 months' imprisonment

Arthur Crabtree [aged 28] (delver) - who was found not guilty

John Horsfield [aged 17] (overlooker) - sentenced to 3 months' imprisonment

Tom Heap [aged 22] (carter) - sentenced to 3 months' imprisonment

Willie Skelton [aged 28] (delver) - who was found not guilty

Jonathan Clayton [aged 30] (delver) - charges against him were withdrawn

After the incident, the Websters moved to Morley and nothing was ever heard from them again. This incident reminded me of a similar occurrence in Silsden some fifteen years later but this time the local Police Station was stoned and besieged by the mad locals.

The village of Mixenden had its own Corn Mill of course. This manorial corn mill, mentioned in 1492 and like the Wheatley Corn Mill, it belonged to the Savile family. It stood on the Halifax side of Mixenden Bridge and the entrance gates still remain. It was used by the Sutcliffe and Priestley families and other owners and tenants have included William Walsh in 1845, Bairstow Brothers [1845-1898], and William Simpson in 1861.

I had now come to the end of this particular historical walk as the bus stop was in sight. Upon checking the timetable I discovered that I had only twenty minutes to wait for the next bus which would take Lou parson and I into Halifax. I sat in the shelter quietly watching a group of lads on mopeds taking the first part of their Motorcycle test in the school yard opposite. As I sat there in the warm afternoon spring sun I shook my head when I realised it was three decades since I had done exactly the same as these lads.

Where have all the years gone?

A Salute to Mr Benton and Mr Woodiwiss

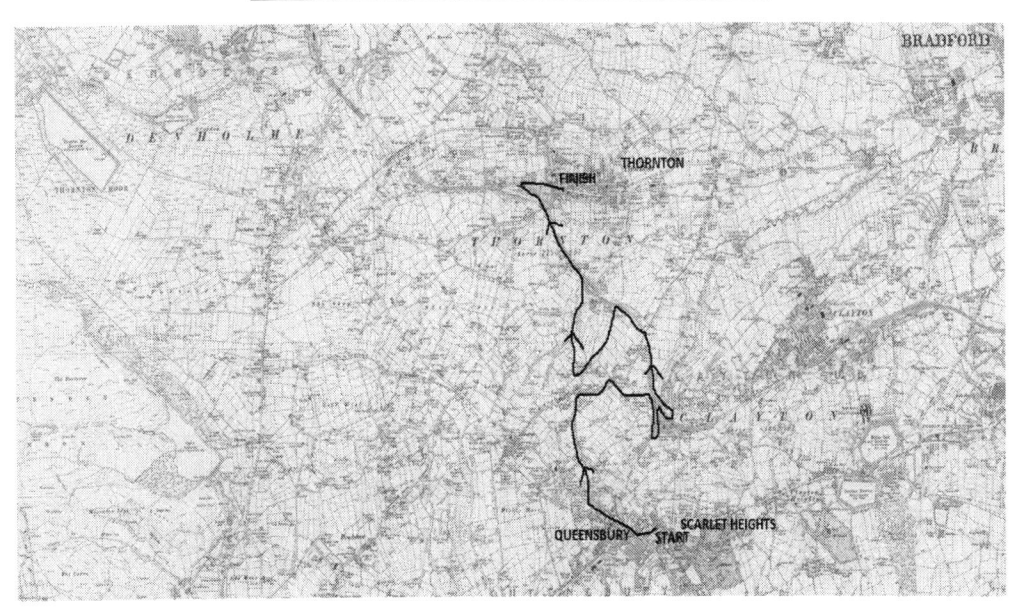

Whilst scouring the old maps for ideas that I could turn into my final historical walk I found myself drawn towards the area of the Queensbury railway triangle. This adventure began with the witnessing of the sun streaking across the land down there and I think it is only right that this book ends with a stroll along its surface.

I had already shot through its centre like an arrow through the heart on one previous walk and caressed the very edge in another as I walked up Station Road. But sitting hunched over the maps it occurred to me that I had yet to complete a walk along the full length of the former railway line, nor had I visited the other historical sites in this particular part of Bradford-dale. So, as usual, I worked out a plan and went out and did it.

Tuesday March 28th was warm and overcast with no sign of rain and there was no rush as I had all day. Lou and I set out from Brickfields and within ten minutes or so we had made good progress along the Brighouse and Denholme Road leading out of the village. Then all of a sudden the ever eager Terrier had steered me down between the cottages at Hill Top and we headed down the tiny footpath named Harp Lane.

Here the track runs down the side of a substantial spoil retaining wall for the former Sandstone quarry that once stood further up the field behind. This quarry was operated by David Knowles who had purchased the land in 1823, and it is claimed that the expense of constructing this vast wall bankrupted him. The quarry was then purchased by Esau Gregson who used it as a private rubbish dump. In 1890 the Council ordered him to desist from "tipping fish, animal and vegetable waste" into his quarry. At the bottom of Harp lane just as it curves back upwards toward the main road there are the remains of a tiny cottage which was known as Harp Bottom. The moss covered stones are just visible in situ in the long grass.

As usual Lou Parson was nosing around in the grass sniffing a trail belonging to some creature of other. Suddenly the silence of the still air was shattered as a Pheasant shot out from literally right under her nose. The dog was stunned for a second as the noble bird made its escape, the snapping canine jaws trailing only a fraction of a second behind. The frantic beating of its wings seemed to reverberate around the hillside as the bird made its lucky escape. Oh well tripe again for tea Lou Parson.

Only a couple of hundred yards away to the right is a row of cottages named Lane Top and beyond here down Bridle Stile Lane stands the cottages of Low Fold. This is quite a historically important building as it was here where the mastermind behind Black Dyke Mills, John Foster, was living when he embarked on his business career. Walking in the other direction from Harp Lane along Carter Lane would lead Lou and I past Carter House and on to the tiny hamlet of Lane Side and West Scholes Gate.

West Scholes was the territory of the Briggs family from the late 1700's and through the 1800's. Apart from a farm, quarries and a brewery the Briggs family also held coal mining rights. Back in Briggs's time Laneside was a road of broken stone and earth, the pavements and kerbs (if any) were constructed of cut stone, with a row of cobbles along the side to prevent erosion when it rained. Gas street lighting was present with the lamps positioned in the road rather than on the pavement.

West Scholes House had originally been three dwellings. The end nearest to Thornton was occupied by John Briggs who began brewing ale in the adjacent sheds. The Briggs family owned most of the land from laneside down towards the brickworks and Birks Wood.

On the other side of Laneside stands a property named Wellfield. This property was erected in 1866 for William Briggs and his wife Agnes. The datestone on the east wall has two Masonic symbols-the compass and square, and the level which may indicate that William was a Senior Warden. It is known that he was indeed a Mason (1861- 1874) in the Harmony Lodge in Bradford.

The Junction Inn made an impression on me as I wandered past, and I bookmarked it for a summers afternoon pint or two in the future. For the time being though I had decided to continue straight on along Cockin Lane towards the three rows of cottages that constitute the hamlet of Yews Green. These typical humble Yorkshire stone buildings stand as proud today as the day they were constructed. Only the weathering of the stone over the past two centuries or so has changed anything down in this veritable time bubble.

It was now time for Lou Parson and I to engage with the railway for the first time today. I wanted to access the famed railway triangle from the path that leads up from Brow Lane to what was Queensbury North Junction. Brow Lane leads past a row of five cottages named Hollingwell Hill. The well after which the dwellings are named stood close by at the edge of the adjacent field.

The substantial stone bridge that once carried the line across Brow Lane stands at the bottom of the hill. The access ramp to Hole Bottom Farm leads off to the left from underneath the bridge, but I turned right and walked up the pathway towards the area which once held so much industrial infrastructure and activity.

Queensbury railway station was a station on the Queensbury lines serving the village of Queensbury above. The station was unusual due to its triangular shape, and at its opening the only other example of this arrangement was Ambergate station in Derbyshire. The station was located some distance away from the town itself, and to further complicate things built at a considerably lower altitude; Queensbury is one of the highest settlements in England and the station was built at around 400 feet lower than the village. Access was via a dimly-lit footpath. There were also three signal boxes at the station, one for each junction on the three station approaches (from Bradford, Keighley and Halifax respectively).

The station was closed to passengers in 1955 and closed completely in 1963. All the station infrastructure has now been demolished with only a small iron service bridge, the tunnel portal and the former Station House remaining. The station area itself has been filled in by inert landfill. Clayton tunnel portal can be found in a large crater that has not been totally infilled just beyond the iron footbridge.

The station was remarkable for having six independent sets of railway offices, all of them typical wooden structure of Great Northern outline which included waiting rooms and lavatories. In addition a booking office and other station buildings stood on an overbridge at the Bradford corner of the triangle. The Bradford to Keighley side of the triangle was carried across a three arch stone and masonry viaduct, and at the Halifax end a subway was provided to connect the four platform ends. The lines were marked with a number of major civil engineering works including several viaducts and tunnels.

The first train pulled in during the spring of 1879. The line north snaked its way to Keighley, embracing viaducts, tunnels and lofty views over the industrial sprawl - earning it the affectionate title of 'The Alpine Route'. To the south-west, via the glorious gloom of Queensbury tunnel, lay Halifax whilst Bradford nestled to the east, also linked by a hole through the hill.

Goods services were minimal and all passenger services were withdrawn on May 22nd 1955, but the station remained open for goods traffic until Nov 11th 1963 although after closure to passengers it was downgraded to an unstaffed public delivery siding. The track was finally lifted back to Horton Park station in June 1966.

Today there is nothing remaining in the triangle area to suggest there was anything here in the past. The substantial viaduct was demolished and the land was completely filled in with landfill.

The tunnel underneath Queensbury itself is blocked by metal gates but access can still be gained as I had heard tales of midnight ravers holding parties inside during the summer months. This tunnel was opened in July 1878 when the link to Halifax was completed. The tunnel was 2501 yards long and ran for almost a quarter of a mile under the village of Queensbury.

It was the longest tunnel on the Great Northern rail system and took nearly four years to complete.

The local topography imposed many constraints on the three lines radiating from Queensbury. Besides the Queensbury tunnel, several other tunnels and viaducts were called for, all a product of John Fraser. Born in Linlithgow in 1819, he was a prolific civil engineer, responsible for numerous lines across Yorkshire's West Riding including sections of the Great Northern's main line to London. As a result, he went on to be appointed as the company's engineer.

Messrs Benton & Woodiwiss, of Manchester and Derby, were contracted to construct the line and all its attendant infrastructure. Work on the tunnel had begun on 21st May 1874. Four observatories were erected, from which a view was commanded over each of the construction shafts. Although eight shafts were originally planned, their spacing was subsequently revised and just seven were initially progressed. Over the years, rumours have persisted that an additional shaft was sunk, presumably to expedite progress through the northern section of the tunnel. If built, there is certainly no sign of it today. Two small apertures in the crown, at around 1,950 yards, have been suggested as its possible location, however consultants working on behalf of the tunnel's owner, British Railways Board (Residuary), assert that no such shaft was ever constructed.

A 10-foot square heading made progress from both ends of the tunnel and the bases of the five shafts, making twelve potential faces in total. A three-shift operation was established, with around 20 men per shaft employed on each. At about 3:40 am on Tuesday 7th December 1875, six miners returned to their working face after retreating to fire shots, under the impression that all had been successful. They discovered however that one had misfired so Henry Jones and John Gough set about withdrawing it. As they did so it exploded, killing them instantly. Another member of the group, John Rowley, was taken to Halifax Infirmary with head injuries and a broken arm, having been initially tended to by works inspector Mr Albrighton.

On Saturday 10th October 1874, 30-year-old Richard Sutcliffe suffered a fatal compound skull fracture when a rope used to haul a cage up No.1 shaft broke, causing it to freefall to the bottom. Masons Herbert Evans and Thomas Dyson were also struck but survived. In May 1876, miner Richard Jones died when a loose rock collapsed onto him. This pattern of tragedy was repeated during construction of all three routes out of Queensbury, resulting in one newspaper christening them "the slaughtering lines"

The following summer brought work to its conclusion and the Great Northern expressed its gratitude by entertaining the 300 men involved to a dinner on 31st July 1878. In late September, a train travelled through the tunnel as part of a preliminary inspection. Major General Hutchinson conducted his examination for the Board of Trade on Wednesday 9th October, deeming railway No.3 unfit for passenger traffic due to the incomplete nature of the works. And so it was a freight only line when the first train enjoyed the 1:100 gradient, descending towards Halifax, on 14th October 1878. Passenger services were eventually introduced in December 1879, after Hutchinson had revisited.

Soon after the tunnel opened, significant defects were detected in the sidewalls, partly as a consequence of poor workmanship but also the mining of coal from a seam immediately adjacent to the tunnel. As a result, January 1883 brought the introduction of a single line running southwards, allowing repairs to take place on the west sidewall. The situation was reversed after 12th May and the work was fully completed in September. As it was regarded as a construction fault, Benton & Woodiwiss were required to bear the cost of carrying out the repairs.

Until recently, the tunnel's northern entrance had been bricked-up, with maintenance access available through steel-plated gates. This arrangement was replaced with a palisade fence following a programme of repair works in 2012. The southernmost half-mile is flooded, reaching roof level at the portal as a consequence of the falling gradient. This accumulation was prompted by the infilling of Strines cutting and the failure to provide a drainage outlet. However pumps have been used to draw off the water when access is required for maintenance.

The north portal is in a poor state, with open mortar joints and bulging stonework. The parapet was lost in the 1980s and the wing walls have almost gone. This deterioration is ongoing, driven by ground movement, the effects of vegetation and cascading water.

As I wandered around the triangle hunger pangs started to attack my belly and I decided it was time to break open the cheese and onion sandwiches. Sitting down in the long grass at the side of what was the Thornton branch of the line I noticed a broken gravestone nearby. A gravestone here, why? It belonged to John Dalby who had worked for The Midland Railway for forty years. Later that night the 1881 census told me that John Dalby was married, age 64, and a Railway Canvasser that lived at number 66, Four Lane Ends in Bradford. He was buried at St John the Baptist in Clayton which was the nearest church to this spot I understand. But exactly why his headstone rests here amongst the tall grass at the former site of the Queensbury railway triangle is anyone's guess.

As I munched on the Old Amsterdam cheese I glanced up towards the skyline at Sharket Head. The tunnel runs under the hill around this point and I knew that the Queensbury Music Centre stands just over the skyline here. This building was of course the Beer House which the Navvies who constructed the tunnel would frequent on a nightly basis whilst they lived in the "Navvy Houses" nearby. These hardened working men came from all corners of the British Isles and many originated from Ireland, so it was only right that strains of Irish folk music began to waft around my consciousness.

Shielding the sun with my hand, my imagination began to conjure up images of filthy and work-stained gnarled men slugging back vast quantities of locally brewed ale. Women were conspicuous by their absence as most of these men had left their wives and families behind. Some men did bring their kin with them when they wandered about seeking employment but these would stay behind to tend to the meagre resources in the Navvy houses close by.

The swishing sound of a passing cyclist brought me back to my senses with a bump. His lycra clad arse protruded high into the air as he peddled like the Devil himself was chasing him. Be gone with you I remarked to no one in particular. It was now time to leave this strange place so I packed my remaining food away and set off back towards Brow Lane. Here I ducked under the bridge and headed for the former entrance to Clayton Fire Clay Works.

Here two rows of quaint old cottages stand on the roadside. The first one is a little back from Brow Lane and the second right on the road itself. Then, after fifty yards or so I came to a most unusual house. Unusual in a sense that it is clad in materials almost totally alien to house building in this area. This house is named "The Elders" and it stands at the entrance to the track which still runs up to another far more substantial house named "The Towers"

Both properties were connected to the owners of the Fireclay Works, The Whitehead family, as were the cottages back down Brow Lane. The Elders itself is faced with glazed brown bricks and heavily embellished with glazed relief products along its front facing wall. Yorkshire stone it most certainly is not!

Lou Parson led me up along the former access track to the Fire Clay Works. Today all traces of this once mighty industrial concern has vanished apart from its tall chimney. Just as the chimney at Black Dyke Mills above serves as a beacon to guide folk back home to Queensbury, this chimney down here also enables you to place yourself in respect to the land.

Julius Whitehead, the founder of the Fire Clay Works constructed for himself a rather grand house just a little further up the track. This property is named The Towers and still stands today. He took possession of the house in 1891 and remained there until his death in 1908. Upon his death, Claude, the youngest son of Julius, took over the running of the business and moved into The Towers with his wife Annie May.

Claude died in 1952 and Annie may in 1963, and soon after the house and gardens were in serious decline. The pool constantly sprung leaks and was drained; the conservatory where their son Harold kept his exotic plants, butterflies and young trout was demolished. Harold died in 1967 and the house was sold to a Mr Clarke, then a couple of years later to a Mr Sharples. It was completely renovated and has changed hands again since. One of Harold's brothers, Vernon, constructed the dome which can be seen on the roof. This was to house the reflecting astronomical telescope which he and Harold had made from scratch.

Julius Whitehead himself established the fireclay works in 1880 to supply the local area with pipework, sanitary products, and chimney pots. The factory exploited a rich seam of clay which ran along Hole Bottom Beck valley and its kilns were fueled by coal brought up from the local pits nearby. He was very inventive and designed and patented amongst other things the Acme Multiple Pipe Making machine. The surviving chimney is said to have been built by Julius's eldest son Claude in a single day, with decorative tiles added later depicting some of the company's products.

The business was started by Julius with the help of his three sons and one daughter, and at its zenith employed over sixty local people. In 1907 the works moved to Cockin Lane because of better clay, and the business was carried on by the next generation of Whiteheads, who started on leaving school, learning to do the whole job themselves whilst continuing to employ local people.

There was not much industrial trouble and only one serious accident in almost 100 years of trading. The kilns were heated to a very high temperature. at which point salt was added to glaze the bricks, and that it was a "sight worth seeing" from Fall Top at night. By December 1969 the demand for these specialised goods had fallen off and, the works being in need of complete refurbishment, it was decided to close them. The men were paid off in December 1969, the works finally closing completely in April 1970.

I had to make my way back onto the former railway track and start the short journey across the valley to Thornton. Thanks to Sustrans the former railway track bed serves today as a nature trail and a cycle cum walking route. It is fairly flat and civilised along its length and a small number of railway bridges still remain. As Lou Parson and I walked along we were passed by no end of cyclists and fellow dog owners who were all taking advantage of this wonderful causeway across the valley.

Crossing over Cocking Lane, the trail was flat and the surrounding countryside just purred by. Lou was startled by a compound of chickens by a small farm. This was right along the side of the trail and if it was not for the wire fencing she would have been in there and no doubt be in her instinctive element with feathers flying everywhere. Crows and Magpies fled the nearby treetops when her high pitched screeching awoke them from their slumbers.

But as flat as this middle section is there are still two fine examples of the type of Victorian civil engineering miracles that Mr Benton and Mr Woodiwiss had to create when they constructed the line. Almost immediately Lou and I were on the top of High Birks Embankment. This 104 feet long, 900 feet long structure was constructed from 250,000 yards of tipping material dug out from the nearby tunnels. Constructed to span the Birks valley and High Birks Beck below, subsidence was a huge problem for the Victorian engineers when it was built.

The second marvellous Victorian engineering masterpiece is Thornton Viaduct. Reaching the beginning of this structure I felt compelled to vault the simple wooden fence and slide down the grassy banking into the valley underneath. I had to see it in its full glory and not just walk along its surface.

After something of a struggle Lou and I stood silently as the viaduct presented itself before us in all its Victorian glory. Pulling the dog to the side I could hardly believe what I was seeing. Never had I witnessed a structure as beautiful as this in all my walks around this area. I felt humble and privileged to stand before this marvel of Victorian ingenuity and engineering. Yes, I was that impressed!

Thornton Viaduct opened in 1878 as part of the Great Northern's route from Queensbury to Keighley - arguably, the most engineered section of railway in West Yorkshire. It is a Grade II listed structure and incorporates twenty barrel vaulted arches - each with a span of forty feet - and its 300-yard length incorporates a rare S-shaped curve to allow access to Thornton Station. The old trackbed crosses Pinch Beck at a height of 120 feet. The structure is formed of 17,000 cubic yards of masonry as well as 750,000 bricks. I felt like staying right where I was and counting every single one.

It is supposedly haunted by the ghost of "Fair Becca", who fell from her horse whilst riding along the top of the viaduct. Local folklore says that if you call her name three times she will appear. This was also the viaduct that was used in the episode of Last of the Summer Wine entitled "Three men and a Mangle." Where they hoisted the mangle up from the road.

I sat there aside the beck for what seemed like hours just gazing at the viaduct. The warm sun beat down upon my bald head, the birds twittered in the nearby trees, and all was well for once. Although it stood perhaps two hundred feet away my eyes examined every stone, every arch, looking for imperfections, but I saw none. Was it really built 139 years ago I said to Lou, it could have been built yesterday? I simply had to get on the top and drink in the scenery below.

So with even greater difficulty than when descending, Lou and I scrambled back up the banking to once again walk along the railway trail. The vista from the top of the viaduct simply took my breath away as the fields, tracks and bare contours of the local topography came to life before me. It was akin to laying a 3D map on a table and standing over it. I could have spent all day simply standing gazing over the parapet of the viaduct but I had an appointment with some real ale.

It has become something of a tradition for me to end each final walk in my books with a visit to a pub and to sink a couple of fine pints of real ale. Drinking is not something I do much of these days as it is proving harder to get things back together the next morning as the years catch up with me. But as I am the boss I can make and change the rules and a couple of pints is about right. My previous book based on the wider Leeds area ended with Lou and I sitting outside The White Horse in Church Fenton late one summer afternoon, and this book ends with us visiting The New Inn in Thornton.

I was joined by two new friends from Yews Green who had arranged to meet me at the pub to talk history and drink real ale. They were amongst the first people from the Queensbury area who got to know Lou and I and made us feel so welcome. I won't name them but I thank you both for your friendliness and kindness.

I cannot recall what beer it was that I had that afternoon, only that it was good and local. It certainly made the setting sun appear more beautiful than usual on the walk back to Scarlet Heights. Once again I struggled up the steep ancient footpath leading from the floor of Bradford-dale up to Sandbeds and stood before the majestic scene that had inspired me to move to Queensbury and write this book in the first place.

Things had come full circle and I think it is pretty apt to end things there.

Made in the USA
Columbia, SC
11 November 2017